COPING

SPIRITUAL·POWER FOR·YOUR·DAILY·LIVING

PAUL R. SCHROEDER

Publishing House
St. Louis

I dedicate this book to the people of God gathered at Our Shepherd Lutheran Church, Greendale, Wisconsin. Their love and support for me and my family is exemplary. Since they reflect the presence of Christ in their lives, it is a joy to serve as their pastor.

Library of Congress Cataloging-in-Publication Data

Schroeder, Paul R. (Paul Reynold), 1933–
    Coping : spiritual power for your daily living / Paul R. Schroeder.

    p.   cm.
    ISBN 0-570-04555-X : $6.95
    1. Christian life—Lutheran authors.   2. Interpersonal relations—Religious aspects—Christianity.   I. Title.

BV4501.2.S2984   1991
248.8—dc20   91-8918

1 2 3 4 5 6 7 8 9 10 MAL 99 98 97 96 95 94 93 92 91

CONTENTS

Preface 4

Acknowledgments 5

Part One: Coping: Our Relationship
with *God* (Spiritual) 7

1. Guaranteed	9	9. New Life	38
2. Help	13	10. Love	41
3. Faith	16	11. Risen	45
4. Obedience	20	12. Scapegoat	48
5. Treasure	23	13. Thanks	51
6. Thomas	27	14. The Gift	53
7. Seeds	31	15. God's Love	57
8. Control	34		

Part Two: Coping: Our Relationship
with *Ourself* (Personal) 60

16. Forward!	62	24. Snapshot	89
17. Salvation	65	25. You	93
18. Goals	68	26. Gifts	96
19. Thorn	72	27. Priorities	100
20. Songs	75	28. Discipleship	102
21. Brain	79	29. Wait	106
22. Serving	81	30. Questions	110
23. Shunammite	85	31. Hope	114

Part Three: Coping: Our Relationship
with *Others* (Relational) 117

32. Show and Tell	119	38. Exclusive	141
33. Quickly	123	39. Commitment	145
34. Someone	126	40. Witness	149
35. Forget	130	41. Victorious	152
36. Mending	134	42. Comfort	155
37. Fishing	137	43. Littleness	158

Preface

My goal in life has been to reach people with God's Word. I believe God's Word contains the answers to all of life's problems and needs. As we apply God's Word to our daily lives, the Holy Spirit strengthens us, our faith grows, and our lives are transformed.

God loves us! He gave us His Son as our Lord and Savior, and He gave us His Word so we can know Him and His will. He wants us to have purposeful and joy-filled lives. By applying His Word to our problems, questions, and needs, we will not only be able to cope, but also lead victorious lives (Rom. 8:37).

The messages in this book were originally published in the monthly newsletter, "Thoughts," which is sent to people who respond to our radio ministry, "The Word Today." God has blessed "The Word Today." The program presently is carried on 143 stations in all 50 states, plus seven foreign countries in three languages. In the past decade, the program has reached 120 million people. Praise be to God!

If this book serves in any way to help anyone, it will be due entirely to God's mercy and grace.

soli Deo gloria
Paul R. Schroeder

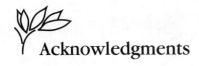

Acknowledgments

I wish to thank the members of the parish I've served for 24 years—Our Shepherd Lutheran Church, Greendale, Wisconsin. Their support and encouragement of my writing is deeply appreciated.

My thanks to my secretary, Carol Fadrowski, who has been a constant source of help and a tireless worker. Special thanks to Russ Larson who has served as adviser and encourager on this project.

And finally, I want to thank my wife Sylvia and my two children, Douglas and Dana, who have encouraged me over the years. I treasure their love.

Paul R. Schroeder

PART 1

Coping: Our Relationship with God

(Spiritual)

1

Guaranteed

We all know how frequently we are "guaranteed satisfaction." Almost any product that is made these days offers a guarantee, and part of that guarantee is that you have to be satisfied with the quality or performance of that product. Whether it's a washing machine or a car, you have to be satisfied that it's performing properly.

Some of these guarantees are pretty good while others leave a lot to be desired. When it actually comes time for you to try to collect on the guarantee, you discover those little clauses which indicate that the manufacturer is not really responsible. You're likely to run into all kinds of exceptions and loopholes. So the guarantee is only as good and reliable as the company that backs it up. If it's a lousy company, the guarantee is meaningless. The company could even be out of business by the time you try to do something about the defective merchandise.

Well, I have a guarantee to offer you that is totally foolproof. There is positively no way that this guarantee can fail. I have titled a beautiful chapter of the Bible, "Satisfaction"— *Isaiah 55*. It is one of the really great chapters of the Bible, which I hope you'll read. While not as significant as Isaiah 53, in my opinion, it is probably one of the 20 most important chapters in the Old Testament. And I realize that is saying a great deal.

Isaiah 55 guarantees you satisfaction! But not the way the world does. Unlike worldly guarantees, it's not limited or restricted in any way. The difference is that the guarantee is made by God! Therefore, it is totally reliable.

Now this beautiful chapter starts out with an invitation that is repeated over and over again. The Lord says,

> Come everyone who is thirsty—here is water! Come, you who have no money—buy grain and eat! Come! Buy wine and milk—it will cost you nothing! Why spend money on what does not satisfy? Why spend your wages and still be hungry? Listen to me and do what I say, and you will enjoy the best food of all.

God is speaking through Isaiah to the children of Israel who have been in captivity in Babylon. They're away from their homeland. It was similar to being in prison. The invitation is *to come*. Their immediate reaction is to say, "But I don't have any money. What am I going to use to buy this food and drink?"

God's answer comes back, "Don't worry. It's as free as a cool breeze on a hot summer day." It's something God is giving you free of charge.

It is necessary to understand that Isaiah is using physical things to describe spiritual blessings. This same sort of thing was done by Jesus when He talked to the woman at the well in Samaria (John 4:1–26). You remember when they were drawing water and Jesus said to her: "If you only knew what God gives and who it is that is asking you for a drink, you would ask Him, and He would give you life-giving water" (v. 10 TEV).

It is that same type of analogy that is being used in Isaiah regarding spiritual food. And there is a parable in the New Testament in which this same teaching is presented. The wedding feast has been prepared, but because the invited guests have declined, the king sends his servants to the highways and byways and "they gathered all whom they found" (Matt. 22:1–10). Paul refers to it another way. He said this is a meal, this is food, a gift that God gives to us by His grace. He says it is not by any of our works, but by God's free gift.

So this "guaranteed satisfaction" that we are talking about is the inner soul finding peace with God through the forgiveness of our sins, the lifting of the burden of guilt, and establishing ourselves as friends of God through His Son, Jesus Christ.

We are told in this important chapter that just as the rain and snow come down (v. 10), and they do not go floating back up into the sky until they have fulfilled the purpose for which they came (mainly to water plants and make them grow), so also the Word of God is not going to return to Him void. It is going to produce a crop which will be harvested. God's Word, this text says, will always produce results (v. 11). It will always accomplish what God intends to do.

Now our job isn't the converting—that's the work of God. Our job is just to get the Word out there. If we put the Word out there and preach the Good News, we know that God will bless, lives will be changed, and people will be reached because God Himself is in charge and blessing with the presence of His Holy Spirit.

As you read Isaiah 55, please note some things that will be helpful in having it become, perhaps, one of your favorites. First of all, notice the price for this satisfaction. The price is nothing, nil, zero, zilch—it's free!

The entire chapter describes a meal that will totally satisfy. Isaiah is referring to spiritual refreshment. The children of Israel are just coming out of captivity and returning to their homeland, and they're invited to receive these things without cost. But even if they had money, they couldn't buy this food because it is not for sale. It is a free gift of God. The giver, who is God in this analogy, doesn't need the money. The entire world is His. He doesn't need anything more. He owns it all. He is God.

This gift of spiritual faith and nourishment, this gift which He offers you and me freely, is the gift of God's love to His people. It is free. Note that there are no restrictions. It doesn't say, "Only certain races may come." It doesn't say, "Only certain ages may come." It doesn't say, "Only those who have accomplished wonderful things may come." It says to *all*—come, come! It's an invitation God still is offering to the whole wide world—*come and believe in My Son, Jesus Christ.*

Notice the promise in verses 6 and 7:

Turn to the Lord and pray to Him, now that He is near. Let the wicked leave their way of life and change their way of thinking. Let them turn to the Lord, our God; He is merciful and quick to forgive (TEV).

I'm perfectly aware that most of our evil deeds flow as a result of evil thought. You are what you think. If you are constantly thinking corrupt and evil things (jealousy, immoralities, greed, etc.), those thoughts eventually lead to actions which are also evil. So he says put away not only your evil actions, but also your evil thoughts. Begin to think in a God-pleasing way. What a marvelous verse to show young people. Fill your thoughts and minds by glorifying and praising God. Spend your time pursuing those things that are pleasing to God.

The whole world around us is so messed up that it is trying to get us to do just the opposite. The world looks for satisfaction in so many ways. It's such a futile thing to follow the world's ambitions. Think of the people who have tried to succeed only to find they are dissatisfied and unfulfilled.

The answer, dear friends, is here in Isaiah 55. Come to God. He will give you "satisfaction guaranteed!" God sent His Son to die for you! He "backed up" His promise. He kept His Word! Now, through Jesus you can have forgiveness of your sins and life eternal. Guaranteed!

2

Help

Psalm 46 begins, "God is our refuge . . ." I'd like you to think of that in terms of *help* which is what it means. God is our help. He is an ever-present help in any time of trouble. Psalm 46 is filled with little phrases that help us focus on the importance of having God as our refuge. Let's look at three of those phrases.

Verse 10: "Be still, and know that I am God." It's hard for us to be still—to be quiet and listen. Sometimes it's good to get away occasionally from all the noise going on around us in today's society.

Have you ever had the opportunity to stand silently in the middle of a desert? Have you looked across the valleys and mountains and taken in a panorama of indescribably beautiful scenery? If you have, like I have, you just know that God is there. You just know that God loves you. Praise God for all that He has done! It's an incredible experience.

If you haven't pulled away from the hustle and bustle of life to meditate and ponder what God has done for you, then I believe you need to remember, acknowledge, and obey this phrase from Psalm 46—*Be still*. Just relax and be quiet and let God reveal Himself to you. Let Him show His majesty and His power to you.

Verse 8: "Come, behold the works of the Lord." Now when you *behold* something you do more than see it. For instance, if you are reading something and your eyes follow along the printed page, but you're not concentrating, then you are only seeing the words. You see the words, but you don't comprehend or behold them.

What God invites you to do is not just look, but *behold—*

13

actually comprehend and understand what it is you are seeing. So here is an invitation from God. Come and behold what He has done. That invitation applies to you and me today. If you are feeling despair and discouragement and you say, "There is no help," then this psalm is for you.

Here is how to go about finding God's help: Be still and let God reveal Himself to you. Do not murmur or complain. Trust in Him.

Open your eyes and look around. See what He has already done.

Hold up your hand and look at it. Praise God if you can still use it. Observe your children. See how they have grown. Observe how God has protected and blessed them. Observe how God has provided for you. You must be alive if you're reading this book. Praise God for that. He has nourished you, supported you, protected you, and here you are. There is still hope. So come and behold what God has done for you. He has not lost control! It may appear that way at times, and it may seem as though everything is desolate and hopeless, but God invites you to open your eyes—especially your eyes of faith—and behold what He has already done for you.

Maybe you're still waiting for help. Then you should take comfort in the words of verse 5 plus these words in the first verse of Psalm 46, He is always "a very present help in trouble."

Verse 5: "He will help right early." The words *right early* caused me to wonder. Could *right early* be a reference to the fact that many, many times throughout the Bible you will notice that God helped in the middle of the night? It's as if to say that the day dawning, the coming of a new day, is what God had in mind.

Remember the account of Joshua at the battle of Jericho? His help came at dawn. (Read Joshua 6:15.) And, of course, one of the most glorious things to remember was the dawning of Easter morning (Matt. 28:1).

Now it's obvious that we shouldn't say that God's help has to come at night or early in the morning. That would be totally misunderstanding the point I'm trying to make. What I am pointing out is that God has frequently offered His help *ahead of time*. He gives His people help at precisely the right moment. Never, ever, has God been late!

Sometimes we feel we have it all worked out. We think that we know just what help is needed and when it should come. We almost end up dictating to God. When it doesn't work out that way, we murmur and complain. We feel sorry for ourselves. But isn't it true that as we look back on our lives we can see that the way God helped us turned out to be best for us in the long run? The truth is that what we felt was right for us at that time in our lives clearly would have been wrong for us.

This beautiful psalm says to us that God is our strength and our refuge. To all who are in trouble, be still and listen for God's kindness. Begin to praise Him and acknowledge His goodness. To help you do that, you must take a look around you and see what God has done for you and praise Him for it.

In times of trouble, sorrow, or pain, turn to Psalm 46 for these reassurances. God will bless you!

3

Faith

Moses was a great man. He is listed among the heroes of faith in Hebrews 11. We can learn from Moses. One of the first things that we notice about Moses is that at certain times in his life, before he was committed to God, he tried to do things *his own way*. You remember how, on one occasion, he saw an Egyptian beating one of his fellow Jews, a slave. He became so incensed that he rushed out and killed the Egyptian. In taking things into his own hands and trying to solve the problem in his own way, he had committed murder. The consequences were immediate. He had to flee for his life, and it brought all kinds of problems upon him.

Later on Moses began to understand that it's important to see things *God's way*. I believe we all desire miracles in our life similar to those that Moses later experienced. We see how powerfully God used him and worked in his life. One of these is mentioned in Hebrews 11 (Faith chapter). It refers to the miraculous crossing of the Red Sea. Because Moses had committed himself to God, God intervened in many miraculous ways: the plagues which led to freedom for the children of Israel, the water emerging from solid rock so that they would have something to drink, the manna and quails which fed them, the durability of their sandals and clothing which lasted for their entire 40-year journey. All are examples of these miracles.

Of course, everyone would like to jump right ahead to the miracles, wouldn't they? They'd like to say, "I'd like miracles to happen in my life. I want to be healed." Or "I want to see this or that happen in my life." But they don't seem to remember that there are important steps that have to occur first. We see these in the life of Moses.

The first step is to see God's will. It's very important to see God's will. But how can you follow God's will if you don't know what it is? So, first of all, you have to see and understand the will of God. You do this by getting into His Word. You do this by prayer—asking Him to reveal His will. Now I am not talking about a specific will in regard to whether you should change jobs or whether you should move, or something like that. Just see how God wants you to live. What is His will for your life? What is your purpose in life, according to God? What has He assigned to you as your most important task to accomplish? We know, of course, that each Christian has been assigned the task of bringing His Word to the world. That's the Great Commission (see Matt. 28:18) given by Jesus and applies to every one of God's people.

Now, how does God want to use you to accomplish that? Work on discovering God's will for your life. One key to that is your faith. You will notice in Hebrews 11 that the phrase "by faith" is repeated over and over again: Verse 23—"By faith Moses when he was born ...." Verse 24—"By faith Moses, when he was grown ...." Verse 27—"By faith he left Egypt ...." Verse 28—"By faith he kept the Passover ...." Faith is the focus, faith is the way that you are in dialogue with God. His Holy Spirit has converted you and brought you to faith. Now, by that faith, discover what God's will is for your life. Once you see that will and know it, then the important thing to do is *to make a choice.*

What good is it to know God's will, to know His commandments, to know His desire for you, and then to choose to walk another way? That's ridiculous! The end result of such a decision is His judgment. But by faith, Moses, as he grew up, (v. 25), made a choice. What were his two options? He could have chosen to follow the way of luxury, the way of all the evil things that were going on in Pharaoh's palace, alienated from God. As a matter of fact, he could have had anything he wanted. Remember when, as a baby, he was found in the bulrushes by Pharaoh's daughter? She adopted him, and he was raised in the royal household where it is likely he grew up with wealth, servants, and prestige. What a fantastic temptation! Or he could choose *God's way.*

In verse 25, Scripture records Moses chose "rather to share ill-treatment with the people of God than to enjoy the fleeting pleasures of sin." Anyone who tells you that there is no pleasure in sin is a fool. We all know better. We all know that Satan has arranged some pleasure in sin. But, it's fleeting, it dissipates, it disappears, it turns to sorrow and grief and despair. The end result is the judgment of the Almighty God. So sin is not the way to go.

Moses made the correct choice. He said, "No, I will not choose to go that way; I will choose to go God's way." Why? Because he wanted a reward from God which would be heavenly. It says in verse 26, "for he looked to the reward." He knew that God would be with him and take care of him and bless him if he chose to go God's way. I believe these first three steps are very important.

1. To see God's will and to know that He put you here on earth to work in His kingdom. He wants to use you to bring His Word to the world. He has a plan and purpose for your life.

2. To consciously make a decision to say, "Yes, God, I will live Your way. I will be obedient to You. I will follow Your will. I do not wish to go the way of the world. I wish to go Your way." Once that choice is made, there remains only one final step.

3. To *continue* to walk in God's will. What good is it if you say, "Well, five years ago I really was following the Lord." What does that have to say about today? Five years ago you might have had faith. What good is that if you have no faith now? The point is if you continue to walk in God's will, He will bless you with His presence, and you will see miracles happen.

Now the world around you may laugh about "miracles" and say, "How can that be?" They may have been in a car wreck in which the car was completely demolished and it's a miracle for anyone to be alive. Yet they might say, "Boy, was I lucky to have that kind of car!" Or "Boy, what a good driver I am!" We know that the people who do not know

God are *spiritually blind*. How can we expect them to see the things of the Spirit? How can we expect them to see miracles?

Yet, those who walk with God and walk in His ways will see how God directs, defends, guides, and protects them. They will see miracles. I am convinced of this in my own life. I plead with you to let this illustration in the life of Moses be an example to you. Let your faith lead you to those three steps.

Review the "Faith" chapter (Hebrews 11), especially verses 23–30, which speaks about Moses. See the will of God, choose the will of God, and walk in the will of God. And you will see miracles!

4

Obedience

Our God tells us that He expects obedience from us. He says, "Those who love Me and keep My commandments are truly My disciples." He speaks of the importance of not only *hearing* the Word of God, but *doing* the Word of God. That means obedience. He speaks all the way through the Scriptures of the importance of "bearing fruit." Being productive, living our faith, and loving one another: all refer to being obedient.

God wants to reach the world with the news of salvation through His Son. Now, God could have done that many different ways. But He chose to use His church, His people, those He has redeemed. He has called us for a great commission. Jesus gave that command to His church just before He ascended into heaven. We find it recorded in Matt. 28:19. "Go therefore and make disciples of all nations, baptizing them in the name of the Father and of the Son and of the Holy Spirit ..."

Unfortunately a lot of people stop there. But that isn't the end of the sentence or the thought. It continues in verse 20, "Teaching them to observe all that I have commanded you." Jesus is speaking of obedience. Not only do we need to *hear* God's Word and *know* it, but to *do* it. Then it closes with that beautiful promise, "And I will be with you always to the close of the age."

I have the feeling that we spend too much of our time teaching and preaching to people's minds. There are people who really know the Word of God. And that's important! But that isn't the end. We also have to reach people's will! The will has to be converted too so that we will *want* to follow God.

The important thing to remember is that obedience comes from God. It is God's presence and His power in our life that will enable us to be obedient. You know that's a tremendous concept if we can just focus on it for a minute and let it sink into us. Under the blessing of God's Holy Spirit, you have to turn your life over to God so that He, working in you, will change your will and create in you a desire to follow Him and serve Him and do good works to glorify His name. It is God's presence in you that prompts obedience.

Now let's say that you have been disobedient. Let's say that you haven't even given it that much thought. You aren't even too concerned about it. Well, what's the first step? The first step—if you are a child of God, and His Holy Spirit is in you—is to recognize that God wants you to *repent*. God calls you to daily repentance. Your sins should not overwhelm you and enslave you so that you revert back to your former way of life. What is the point then? If you live sinfully disobedient lives, then your religion and your Christianity are some sort of fake. On the one hand you are pretending to love God and serve Him. On the other hand, you're living a worldly and sinful life.

God wants us to repent and come back to Him. That's why we need to daily live with the Lord Jesus Christ and His forgiving love. That's why we daily need God's Word. That's why we need the fellowship of Christians who can support us and strengthen us. These Christian friends will reprimand us when we are wrong and call us back when we go the wrong way. This is necessary so that God works in our heart and mind and prompts us to obedience.

I think we need to do more teaching on obedience. We teach the commandments. We teach the will of God. We teach the Scriptures. Yet, there are many Christians who are filling our churches who seem to think that the whole thing is "just talk." They think, "Sure, we say that. Sure, we teach that. But we know that nobody can live that way. We know that nobody does that. We know that everybody has a double standard and if you really live that way, you would really be an oddball in the world. People would not want you around because you'd be so different from everyone else."

See how Satan tries to get us to offer excuses why we are not obedient. We can go on and on like that, and all the time we do we are *unrepentant*. We are not really changing our will because we have not turned it over to God. God wants our hearts to be moved and changed. He wants us to become His people. He wants us to become the sort of people who will be usable to Him. He wants to change the world by bringing His Gospel to all people. We have to make a decision! "Choose you this day whom you will serve."

How committed are you? Jesus was always inviting people to follow Him. He always gave them an option. Do you remember the rich young ruler who talked with Him? Jesus explained what the commitment involved. The young ruler went sadly away. The text does *not* say that Jesus ran after him and began negotiating, "Would you consider going half-way? How about going 20 percent?" No! The man walked sadly away. As far as we know, he never did return to the Lord.

You can be sure when God moves people to say, "Yes," then you really have something! If God has called them, if God moved them to respond, then it's God's job. God will keep them going. God will inspire them. God will enable them. God will use them. God blesses! God does the motivating. God does the enabling.

I believe it is an incredible thing to watch God at work through His people. If people join together committed to the cause of serving the Lord, God can use them in a mighty way. I believe God wants to work in ways that the Christian church has not yet completely understood. I believe that if we would commit ourselves and really work together on a common goal, there would be no limitation on what we could do for God. When God is doing it, there is no limitation. God can do all things.

So whatever God is saying or doing in your heart, listen to Him. Turn away from sin, confess it, repent of it, and ask God's forgiveness. You know He loves you! He wants to make you happy. He wants to work in your heart and in your will. He wants to make you His disciple. He wants you to become a partner in reaching the world with His Word.

Treasure

When we were children we sometimes played treasure hunt or scavenger hunt. It was a thrilling, exciting game. Everyone was given a list of odd or unusual articles that were difficult to find. We had to go to homes or businesses, and everyone would be racing against the clock to see who could gather most or all of these "treasured" items. If you found them all, you or your team were the winners.

Even adults hunt treasures. In fact, you can buy magazines about treasure hunting at the newsstands. Metal detectors are available that beep to indicate buried coins or metal underneath the soil. I imagine everyone thinks about how exciting it would be to find a treasure.

Well, the Bible uses our curiosity and our natural tendency to want to find treasure to illustrate what the kingdom of heaven is like. In Matthew 13, six parables speak about the kingdom of God.

The kingdom of God is like:

> A man who sowed good seed ... (v. 24)
>
> A grain of mustard seed ... (v. 31)
>
> Leaven ... (v. 33)
>
> Treasure hidden in a field ... (v. 44)
>
> A merchant in search of fine pearls ... (v. 45)
>
> A net ... (v. 47)

Jesus had been teaching the parables to the multitudes. Then He became more personal and talked to just His disciples (v. 36). He said that there is such a thing as spiritual treasure and, obviously, it is different from earthly treasure. In fact, quite frequently earthly treasures can hinder one from finding the spiritual treasure.

What is this spiritual treasure? The Bible says:

> Do not lay up for yourselves treasures on earth, where moth and rust consume and where thieves break in and steal, but lay up for yourselves treasures in heaven, where neither moth nor rust consume and where thieves do not break in and steal. For where your treasure is, there will your heart be also (Matt. 6:19–21).

> Sell your possessions, and give alms; provide yourselves with purses that do not grow old, with a treasure in the heavens that does not fail, where no thief approaches and no moth destroys. For where your treasure is, there will your heart be also (Luke 12:33–34).

> Indeed I count everything as loss because of the surpassing worth of knowing Christ Jesus my Lord. For His sake, I have suffered the loss of all things, and count them as refuse, in order that I may gain Christ (Phil. 3:8).

> As for the rich in this world, charge them not to be haughty, nor to set their hopes on uncertain riches but on God who richly furnishes us with everything to enjoy. They are to do good, to be rich in good deeds, liberal and generous, thus laying up for themselves a good foundation for the future, so that they may take hold of the life which is life indeed (1 Tim. 6:17–19).

So the spiritual treasure is *coming to faith,* discovering Jesus Christ as our personal Lord and Savior, and the joy which that brings.

In Matt. 13:44, we are told about a man who is walking in a field and stumbles upon a treasure. One of the things you have to realize is that this parable doesn't necessarily say that he was out there *looking* for the treasure. The Samaritan woman at the well in John 4:7–26 was not seeking. As a matter of fact, Jesus confronts her right there on the spot. And St. Paul surely was not seeking to find Jesus prior to his conversion. (Read Acts 9.)

It's probably true that those who are not seeking—those who are just kind of hit over the head, so to speak, in terms of God coming and rescuing them—find a first-love excitement or joy. They are filled with a desire to serve God. Too often that first-love enthusiasm and joy are cooled by a complacency that develops in some people after they have been Christians for decades. They have lost their eagerness to do the Lord's will.

But there are those who search. The classic example is Nicodemus. (Read John 3.) The merchant also was searching for a fine pearl (Matt. 13:45). We, too, searching or not, often go through life aimlessly. But when we find Christ, when we come to faith, we are ready to give up everything because that pearl—faith in Jesus Christ—has greater value. Or to put it differently—if you're already a Christian and you gain a deeper insight into your Christianity, your faith grows more meaningful. You're drawn closer to Christ. You have found a pearl to which nothing else can compare. There is a lot to be learned in these two parables of the kingdom of God: the treasure found in a field and the discovery of the pearl of great price.

In Matt. 13:47–50 we read the parable of the dragnet with an explanation. We can know exactly what is meant. The net, or seine, was probably very high and very long. More than likely one end was fastened to a tree or stake on the shoreline. Then it was let down into the water by a boat. The fishermen carefully worked the net back toward the shore so that it picked up every kind of fish. As a matter of fact, even the dead fish would be caught up in this net. You notice that a selection is then made. This is a reference to the final judgment that will take place in the kingdom of God—the "good" into vessels, the "bad" thrown away. There is no "in-between." It's either good or bad. Either heaven or hell. There is no other possibility.

Here are some further references to the "bad," those who reject Jesus Christ:

> The end of those things is death (Rom. 6:21).
>
> Their end will correspond to their deeds (2 Cor. 11:15).
>
> Their end is destruction, their god is the belly, and they glory in their shame, with minds set on earthly things (Phil. 3:19).
>
> But if it bears thorns and thistles, it is worthless and near to being cursed; its end is to be burned (Heb. 6:8).
>
> For the time has come for judgment to begin with the household of God; and if it begins with us, what will be the end of those who do not obey the gospel of God? (1 Peter 4:17).

God's judgment and wrath will be carried out on those who do not believe in Jesus. Those who reject Him are rejecting His offer of forgiveness.

But this parable also reveals that God will save those who have faith. Those who know Jesus Christ and believe in Him are pronounced righteous by God. They are called good because they have been washed in the blood of the Lamb—Christ Himself.

> ... you remember that ever since you were a child, you have known the Holy Scriptures, which are able to give you the wisdom that leads to salvation through faith in Christ Jesus (2 Tim. 3:15 TEV).
>
> The Son of Man came to seek and to save the lost (Luke 19:10 TEV).
>
> For God loved the world so much that He gave His only Son, so that everyone who believes in Him may not die but have eternal life (John 3:16 TEV).

6

Thomas

Thomas, you'll recall, was one of the Lord's disciples. He was among those who doubted the resurrection of Christ. Now, we all know that doubts occur in the lives of Christians. And doubts occurred in the lives of each of the disciples at various times. Doubts occurred in the mind of John the Baptist too.

If your Christian friends are honest, they'll tell you that they've also had doubts. Doubts need to be resolved and brought to the Lord and turned into a conviction of faith. Many people look upon doubts as though they are expressions of unbelief—as if they indicate that they are no longer believers in Jesus Christ. That certainly is not true!

The real question of whether or not you are a child of God, in relation to your doubts, is how you handle your doubts and what you do with your doubts. If the doubts become a matter of pride, and you intellectualize them and go around trying to stump other people with questions that you believe are unanswerable, and in a secret way you pride yourself on your intellect and your ability to find what you would call "loopholes" and "problems" in the Word of God, then it's apparent that the doubts are leading you directly toward unbelief. You are nourishing them. As a matter of fact, you're quite proud of them. Now, on the other hand, if your doubts are troublesome and burdensome, and you want them resolved and bring them to God and ask for His blessing— and you ask for His strength and the power of His Spirit to enable you to have them resolved—then you are dealing with your doubts in the right and proper way.

We see some of Thomas' problems in John 14. Jesus is preparing His disciples for the fact that He is going to be leaving them and ascending into heaven. He is returning to be with His Father. So, in that beautiful chapter, which is one of the key chapters of the Bible, He says, "I am going to prepare a way for you." He goes into detail. Thomas jumps in and says, "Now wait a minute. We don't know the way and how can we know where You are going?" Jesus answered in that beautiful, comforting sentence, "I am the Way, the Truth, and the Life." Jesus explains there is no way to come to the Father except through Him. He is the Way, and the Truth, and the Life.

To learn a little more about Thomas and the situation in which his doubts occurred, turn to John 20. Beginning with verse 24, we see that apparently Thomas, for one reason or another, was missing some fellowship with the other disciples. Perhaps he had some kind of emergency. Or he might have had something to do that he felt was more important than attending the prayer meeting. Because of his absence, he missed the appearance of the resurrected Lord.

Many people today have become disenchanted with the organized church. Maybe they don't like the pastor. Maybe they don't like some of the members. Or they have found some other excuse (and that's really what they are—excuses) for not attending the worship and the fellowship at their local congregation. I believe that is equivalent to what Thomas did. He missed the prayer meeting. You don't know what God has in mind for you at the next church service or prayer meeting. In a special way, God may appear to you—out of His Word, and the message that is proclaimed. He might meet a need or a doubt. He wants to help you, but you have to be there. You can go along for awhile not really being hit by anything extraordinary or overwhelming at church. Then all of a sudden, on a certain day, something really hits you and you praise God. Because you were there, it was really a tremendous help to you.

Thomas wasn't impressed by the witness of the other disciples. He had to see for himself. He must have been in a pretty sad state of affairs. At any rate, he did come to the next prayer meeting. Jesus once again appeared and He went over to Thomas and challenged him, "Put your finger here, and look at my hands; then stretch out your hand and put it in my side. Stop your doubting and believe!"

Here was a very direct challenge and confrontation by Jesus Christ to Thomas. We have to remember, as we deal with people who have doubts and who are struggling with their faith, that there is *only one solution*. It's not intellectual. It's not that we have to sit for hours and argue the point and hope that something will "click" in their mind. And it's not emotional. It's not that we have to build up such a head of steam that we get them all supercharged up until all of a sudden in a frenzy of emotion they will wail and moan and say, "Oh, now I understand and believe." No. It's not that. Because it's not from a human origin that our doubts can be resolved. The only way that doubts can be resolved is by the power of God's Holy Spirit!

We are told that the way in which we release God's Holy Spirit to work faith in our hearts is to proclaim and confront people with Jesus Christ. The simple fact is that we have to confront them with Jesus Christ. Who do you say He is? Do you see the nail prints in His hands? Do you see that He suffered and died as your Savior? Do you see His pierced side where water and blood flowed out? Do you see that His death is for your forgiveness?

Then, under the power of God's Holy Spirit, your doubts will be resolved and removed. You will be brought again to a position of faith and conviction. That is exactly what happened to Thomas. He was confronted by Jesus Christ! He comes back to faith and says, "My Lord and my God!" We read that confession in John 20:28. What a beautiful confession! "My Lord and my God!"

Take a close look at the things that are keeping you from God's house and worshiping at His holy Christian church in your community. Maybe it has been a doubt that has never been resolved. Maybe something has been troubling you that you've never come clean with and have never discussed with your Lord. It's high time that you bring this to Him. Tell Him your fears, your worries, and your troubles. He will resolve them. He will restore you to faith. That is His will. If you will simply come to Him, He will reveal Himself to you just as He did to Thomas. You will be restored in your faith.

Do not be a Thomas who is absent and away from the fellowship. You're not going to get any help that way because you are out of touch with God's Holy Spirit. He works in His holy Christian church. I urge you to come back to that prayer meeting or that church service or to that fellowship gathering with your fellow believers. Let God's power and the power of His Spirit work in you. Your doubts and your needs will be met. Together with Thomas, you will again confess Him before people, and your doubts will be removed. Your conviction of faith will express with Thomas as you speak of Jesus, "He is *my* Lord and *my* God!"

7

Seeds

Spring is a terrific time of year. It's a time when many people plant seeds in a vegetable or flower garden. What a joy it is to see those seeds sprout and grow. It's positively phenomenal, isn't it? Isn't it incredible what's inside a seed? It can become a plant or a vine or a bush or a tree. It's really amazing how God has put into effect all of the principles of growth. Isn't it interesting that the seed has to decay and die first in order to take on a new shape and become a new image of whatever that seed is going to produce?

God's entire creative process is overwhelming! You'd have to be a fool to say there is no God.

Seeds are used in the Bible to teach us certain things. One of the ways in which the example of the seed is used is to show us we will reap what we sow. It is always true. If you sow corn, you are going to get a field of corn. If you sow wheat, you'll get a field of wheat. Never, ever, does that vary. In other words, you'll never get a field of wheat if you've sown corn. You will always get a crop of the seed you've sown.

Scripture uses that as a principle of life. If we sow hatred and jealousy, and if we are sarcastic and filled with negative thoughts, inflicting them upon our family and children, then we are going to reap the results. We shouldn't be surprised if our children grow up to be suspicious, unhappy, negative, or fearful. We reap exactly what we sow.

I think one of the most important points to realize is that sin bears its own fruit. Most of the sins you can think of— whether they be spiritual, moral, physical, or psychological— result in destruction. To illustrate that point, let's say a person is constantly getting drunk. It's not surprising if the result of that sowing is the reaping of a disease called cirrhosis of the liver. The body has been abused for so long and so violently that disease results. If not disease, then it might be a car accident or a son or daughter who becomes an alcoholic. In 2 Cor. 9:6–8, we read:

> Remember that the person who plants few seeds will have a small crop; the one who plants many seeds will have a large crop. Each one should give, then, as he has decided, not with regret or out of a sense of duty; for God loves the one who gives gladly. And God is able to give you more than you need, so that you will always have all you need for yourselves and more than enough for every good cause (TEV).

These verses deal with a subject many people in the church are confused about—giving. More people are offended and turned off and change churches because of this subject. In the verses you've just read, and in many other parts of the Bible, God addresses the subject of giving. He says, "If you plant a few seeds you'll have a small crop; if you plant many seeds you'll have a large crop." It's so elementary, so basic, yet people get all twisted up on this subject. It's almost as if Satan wants to wave all kinds of red flags in front of them.

Maybe some of you are feeling apprehensive right now because you're subconsciously aware that God is speaking to you so that you will understand Christian giving. God says you cannot out-give Him. If you want to be richly blessed, then give abundantly. Give wholeheartedly. Give sacrificially. He will bless you accordingly. Let's review 2 Cor. 9:7:

> Each one should give, then, as he has decided, not with regret or out of a sense of duty; for God loves the one who gives gladly (TEV).

Now isn't that beautiful? God is saying that if you understand the principle involved, then you will be a cheerful giver. Don't give reluctantly or grumblingly, or because you "have to."

Keep in mind that your attitude affects your children's attitude too. If all they hear every Sunday morning is griping and complaining and sarcastic comments like, "All the church is interested in is our money," what impression of giving do your children get? No wonder many children grow up with a negative attitude towards giving to God. As a result, they forfeit so many of His blessings. Because they sow sparingly, they reap sparingly. This profound teaching of Scripture is so simple even a child can understand it.

We know that there are insects and diseases that attack trees and plants. So after planting the seed, there has to be protective care and nourishing. The seed has to be watered, fertilized, and sprayed with insecticide.

In the same way in Matthew 13 we're told about the seed of God's Word as it is planted. There are many ways in which Satan tries to stamp out that seed to keep it from growing. Even right now, in your own heart, there is a struggle going on. If Satan can stamp out your faith and keep you from growing and making a commitment to God, then it will wither, and you're right back where you started.

But God offers to all His people the *healing* process through repentance and forgiveness. Let the "spraying" of Jesus' blood cleanse you. Through Him we have the forgiveness of all our sins. Through Him we are washed clean. And if we feed and nourish on Him, His forgiveness, His love, His Spirit, we will grow healthy and strong spiritually.

John 15:1–11 speaks of those who live in Jesus Christ as being *abundant* in their bearing good fruit. In this very simple and understandable way, Scripture teaches us about spiritual life—what it should be, how it should grow, how it should be nourished and taken care of—and how it should produce fruit to the glory of God.

I hope that you will take a step forward in your giving and become a generous sacrificial giver so that you will see more and more of the blessings and reap what God will give you.

8

Control

Let's reflect on the Christian life. We know there are many people within the church who claim to be Christians, yet they do not give a very strong Christian witness to the community. Let's look at this problem, see what causes it, and hopefully, through God's Spirit, find a solution.

I'd like to begin by having you read Gal. 5:25: "If we live by the Spirit, let us also walk by the Spirit." He has given us life—and He must also control our lives. That's a very important point. When you've come to faith in Christ, that's beautiful, that's wonderful—but where is the evidence of that faith? There is need for *control.* The Scriptures tell us that the control, or dominating influence, in the Christian life has to be the Spirit of God. He has to be present in us. He is to *control* what we say, what we do, and how we live.

Now frequently the conversion of a person is referred to as "Christ coming to live in the heart." The throne of your heart, as the Campus Crusade people refer to it, has a new occupant. Instead of you sitting on the throne and saying that you're in charge, Christ comes onto that throne. He now lives there and rules and controls. That's a nice way to think about it, and it's helpful too.

You know, it's one thing to own a piece of property, such as a house, and just "stop in" every now and then. If it's used primarily as a sleeping place, you wouldn't call it a home, would you? Children who grow up in that kind of a house aren't going to have too good an understanding of a real home. A real home should have love, warmth, and togetherness.

In the same way, it seems some people invite Christ into their hearts and then just want Him to "pop in" every now and then. They want God to "just stop over for a little while, but then be on His way again." This is very different from what the Bible says about the indwelling Spirit of God. That indwelling is, instead, a condition that resembles more a feeling of being at home with God—not just popping in and out—but an ongoing relationship where the home is so loving and wonderful that the individual longs to be part of what is going on there. So our heart is not a "pop in" place for Jesus. Instead, it is to be a home in which He feels comfortable. Because He lives in us, we reflect Him. He is in control. He is in charge. Our thinking and doing become Christlike because of His being at home in our hearts.

Using the analogy of a home, let's apply it to some rooms. Suppose Christ is living in our heart, and He walks around our house. He goes into the library and sees what we are reading. Would He feel uncomfortable? Maybe we need to clean out the library in order for Jesus to feel more at home.

Or suppose He went into the kitchen. Would He see things there that would grieve Him? Would He find illegal drugs? Are we gorging ourselves with food? Whatever the sin or problem, let's seriously ask ourselves, "Would Jesus feel at home in our kitchen?"

What about the living room? Do family members have time to sit down and chat? Or have we become too busy like so many families? Jesus made it clear that He wants us to talk things over with Him—to come to Him with our concerns and needs and problems.

Just think, we have the resource of God's Holy Spirit at our disposal. The Spirit of almighty God will help us cope with our problems, needs, difficulties, and worries. The all-divine, all-powerful Spirit of God lives and dwells within us.

If you believe that Jesus Christ is your personal Savior, then you've been converted. You are a member of the Christian family. You have been forgiven, cleansed, and given the gift of eternal life. Now grow in that relationship, become stronger in that relationship. Apply His thinking and His presence to your every need and problem, every situation in your daily life. Check out the "home" in your heart. Go through the rooms one by one and see whether they are places where

Jesus will feel comfortable. If they are not, ask for His help to clean them up.

> Ah, dearest Jesus, Holy Child,
> Make Thee a bed—soft undefiled—
> Within my heart that it may be
> A quiet chamber kept for Thee.

If your heart is that kind of place, you will feel more and more of the indwelling Spirit of God. You will become stronger and stronger, more and more committed. It is that growth that needs to take place within the lives of Christians. We need to have stronger, more committed children of God. We will not be defeated by adversity or trouble. We will stand firm.

The Bible talks of "trees planted beside a river." The roots have sunk down deeply into the soil and spread out. Therefore they bear fruit:

> (The man who delights in the law of the Lord ...) he is like a tree planted by streams of water, that yields its fruits in its season, and its leaf will not wither. In all that he does, he prospers (Ps. 1:3).

> (The man who trusts in the Lord ...) he is like a tree planted by water, that sends out its roots by the stream, and does not fear when heat comes, for its leaves remain green, and is not anxious in the year of drought, for it does not cease to bear fruit (Jer. 17:8).

And Jesus speaks of two kinds of people: Those who build on sand (the storms come, erosion takes place, and the house crumbles), and those who build squarely upon a rock. In storms and troubles, that foundation is going to stand. In Matt. 7:24–27 we read:

> Everyone then who hears these words of mine and does them will be like a wise man who built his house upon the rock; and the rain fell, and

the floods came, and the winds blew and beat upon that house, but it did not fall, because it had been founded on the rock. And everyone who hears these words of mine and does not do them will be like a foolish man who built his house upon the sand; and the rain fell, and the floods came, and the winds blew and beat against that house, and it fell; and great was the fall of it.

So, first Christ must come into our life and make Himself known to us so that we believe in Him as our personal Lord. Then, as we grow and mature, we make use of all the things that are available to us:

Let not sin therefore reign in your mortal bodies, to make you obey their passions. Do not yield your members to sin as instruments of wickedness, but yield yourselves to God as men who have been brought from death to life, and your members to God as instruments of righteousness (Rom. 6:12–13).

Therefore take the whole armor of God, that you may be able to withstand in the evil day, and having done all, to stand. Stand therefore, having girded your loins with truth, and having put on the breastplate of righteousness, and having shod your feet with the equipment of the gospel of peace; above all taking the shield of faith, with which you can quench all the flaming darts of the evil one. And take the helmet of salvation, and the sword of the Spirit, which is the word of God. (Eph. 6:13–17).

This armor of God is offered to us as we go into daily battle. God wants to be with us constantly. When He is present and controlling our lives, it's going to show up in ways that people will notice. What a tremendous influence we will be to people around us as Christ dwells more and more in our hearts.

9

New Life

Those who believe in Jesus Christ have been given a "new life." I have several favorite Bible verses that deal with the subject. The first is Gal. 2:20. It speaks about this *new life* that we have in Jesus Christ—this new birth. The other is John 3:1–6. Jesus is talking with Nicodemus about the need to be born again. But the one I prefer on this subject is in Romans 6, especially the first 13 verses.

We know that Paul, who wrote the letter to the Romans, knew full well the difference and the extreme conflict between what he was formerly, and what he had become by the power of Christ at his conversion. This "before" and "after" picture is one way we can describe the *new life*.

Maybe it would be helpful to first look at some definitions. How can you be sure that you are in this *new life*, and that you have this *new life*? The most important point of all is that you accept Jesus as your personal Savior. Now, that is different than merely saying you believe He lived on earth. You could, of course, say that historically about Napoleon, Julius Caesar, or anyone else. But when you say that you accept Jesus as your personal Savior, it means that you trust in Him for your salvation—you believe that there is no other way to have the forgiveness of your sins, and you know that there is no other way to be saved but through Him. That is what it means to be a Christian and have the *new life* of God's Spirit living in you.

Another thing you can look at is your attitude toward God. Do you come to God with a defiant attitude? Do you say things like, "Well, if God is fair, He is going to save me because I am certainly better than a lot of people I know."

That kind of "I deserve it" attitude is not pleasing to God and reveals that the *new life* is not in you. When we come to God, we should come with a repentant heart, asking for forgiveness of our sins. God expects us to humble ourselves before Him and to recognize that we do not *deserve* His mercy or His grace. He freely gives us the gift of salvation out of love, not because we deserve it.

Are you coming to God defiantly or humbly? That will give you an indication of whether the *new life* is in you.

Also, you can look at how willing you are to confess Him before people. There are two important verses that speak of this in Scripture. One is Rom. 10:9–11. The other is Matt. 10:32–33. In both places it tells us that whoever confesses Jesus before people will be confessed by Jesus before His Father. Now the point is that if God's Holy Spirit is living within you, you will confess Him to other people. The presence of God's Spirit within you will make it impossible for you to keep that information private as if it were only your little secret. God intends us to proclaim our faith in Him and to hold up Jesus before other people. So you can take a look at that and see whether or not you are within the *new life*.

A frequent theme in the Bible is *growth*. That is true of all things that God has created. It's true of birds, animals, fish, and all plants—vegetables, grass, weeds, trees, etc. And it's true of human beings. When you stop growing, you are dead. Everything alive must grow to stay alive! Now, it is a very important thing to realize that the Bible also speaks of *faith* as being alive and growing. Another way to look at your *new life* is to see whether or not you are still growing. Are you walking day by day with Jesus Christ? Is your prayer life growing? Is your worship life growing? You should be striving every day to please God and walk in His ways. In our *new life* we are to be imitators of Jesus Christ.

Of course, there are also responsibilities connected with this *new life*. We are told as Christians that we are to worship, pray, fellowship with believers, and to spread God's Word. It usually is a handful of God's faithful people who do the majority of the work. You can talk to any pastor and he will tell you that 90 percent of whatever is accomplished by his parish is done by about 10 percent of the people.

Now praise God that things are being done—missionaries are being sent out, broadcasts are being aired—but isn't it sad when we think of what could be done if more of God's people would respond and really help? At some point you have to ask yourself, "Am I part of the *problem* or part of the *solution*?" I hope that God will move you to become a part of the solution. God is asking you to join hands with fellow believers in carrying out His command to reach the world for Him.

In addition to defining this *new life* and pointing out some of its duties, I want to tell you about its benefits. Those who have "new life" have peace in their heart. Just think of the joy and peace that God gives to all who believe in His Son, Jesus Christ. Peace! You know that is one thing that everyone wants. To be at peace with God and with our fellowman.

It is an enormous gift from almighty God to know that your sins are forgiven, to be certain that your guilt has been washed away. If you were to die this very second, you will be saved if you believe in Jesus Christ as your Savior. You will have eternal life. This *new life* that Jesus Christ has given you is not only to produce *joy* here, and the peace that we just mentioned, but also eternal joy. It does not end at the moment of physical death. It is a life that goes on forever!

Jesus has promised us that He is going to return again. Now if you die before His return, you will nevertheless be with Him and your body will be resurrected on Judgment Day. You will live eternally with Him. If you are still alive when Jesus returns, you will be changed in an instant. Your sinful body will be transformed into a holy body. It will be the same you—the same person, but without sin. This new life that Jesus is living within you today, by the power of God's Holy Spirit, will be a life that will never, never end. We will be before the throne of God forever.

Our "new life" in Christ is for now and forever. Praise God!

10

Love

Once in a while someone will try to show how loving he or she is by making a statement like: "If I were God, I wouldn't damn anyone." Or you will occasionally hear someone try to be very profound and say, "If God is so loving, how can He damn someone who never had a chance to hear about Him?" In other words, it would not be fair of God to do that. In their opinion, they would be even more loving than God. If they were God, they would save everyone. Such thoughts are blasphemous because those people are setting themselves up as being more loving than God. But God in His very essence is *love*!

So let's think this through and see what it is that we are actually working with when we talk about the fairness and justice of God. We are told that God is holy. He is without sin, totally fair, totally just. He would have the right, humanly speaking, to damn everyone to hell. The mystery is not that God damns anyone; the mystery is that He saves anyone!

From Scripture it is perfectly clear why God, in His wrath, could condemn every human being. It is clear to me that God would have every right to damn me. Certainly there is nothing of my own worth or goodness that I could hold up to God and say, "Look, God, you have to save me because I'm one of your preachers. I'm a good husband and father. I don't cheat or steal or swear. I give you a lot of my earnings." There is no way that I (or you) could be saved by God unless, in His mercy and love, He offered us the way to salvation as His gift to us—which, of course, is what He has done in His own Son, Jesus Christ.

So the key point is not that there is a mystery in God's

wrath, but rather the mystery is that He and His love are going to save *anyone*. That is exciting because it boils down to the fact that He has given the gift of faith to every believer in Jesus Christ. The incredible thing is that He is going to save those who believe in Christ.

Now let's think for a moment about a person who has a large dog that he is trying to train. He loves that dog and is going to train it to bring back a stick. He throws the stick, the dog runs after it, fetches it, and brings it back. But instead of handing his master the stick, he bites his master's hand. Well, that would be a little bit disconcerting and terribly uncomfortable. Let's imagine the owner would say, "Well, after all, it's the first mistake the dog has made, and I won't get too upset about it. I'll try it again." So, with the other hand, the person throws out the stick; the dog runs and brings it back. But again, instead of handing it to the master, he savagely bites the other hand. Now, I don't care how loving that person is, at this point he would want to get that dog out of his sight. All of his loving feelings would disappear, and he would tell himself, "Get rid of this dog! Look at what he's doing to me!" Now keep that thought in mind because I'll come back to it later.

In the early 1970s I met the late Colonel Sanders at the St. George Hotel in Jerusalem where we were both staying. He heard me lecturing to the tour group that I'd brought to the Holy Land. I was reviewing the things we'd seen that day. Colonel Sanders came over and said, "Young man, you seem to know quite a bit about this area of the world." I told him I'd been there before, and I knew a few things about it. He asked if we could talk, so we sat down and talked for about an hour. But the reason I'm mentioning our meeting is because he was dressed totally in white except for his black bow tie. He looked just exactly like the pictures you've seen of him—white suit, white shoes, white socks, even white hair, and a white goatee. His clothes were spotlessly clean, very neatly pressed, very immaculate.

Now, just think what a terrible thing it would be if Colonel Sanders was standing on a curb in Jerusalem and a bus came by and splashed mud all over him. Can you imagine that? Mud all over his white suit.

Or think about a bratty child taking a water pistol and filling it with ink and squirting it all over the colonel's white suit. That would be intolerable, wouldn't it?

Now, let's get back to our discussion about our holy and righteous God who also hates and abhors sin. He will not tolerate sin. He does not accept sin. Sin is not going to be permitted in His heavenly kingdom. To a holy, righteous, totally perfect God, sin is an abomination.

To God our sin is like the dog biting the master's hands that we described earlier. Instead of being gentle and obedient, the dog rebels and bites his master. He isn't remembering his master's love and patience, his goodness and providence. And think of that in terms of our coming to the almighty God and shaking our little human fist in His face and saying, "Well, God, I don't want to do it Your way. I'll do it my way." How many times would you "take it"? How long do you think it would be before you gave up on that creature (that you created) who rebelled and ignored your goodness?

The Bible talks about the heart of God being grieved and about the sorrow of God when He sees our rebellion and our unfaithfulness and our sinfulness. And yet we come every day and say, "I'll do it my own way." That is what sin is. We are telling God that we want our way instead of His. And we often do that willfully and with determination. Let me tell you, it would be perfectly fair if God would at some point simply stamp us all out! He would say, "Okay, enough is enough! I've had it with you. Who do you think you are?" Then He would zap us! That would be perfectly logical. And God would be totally fair in doing that.

No, the amazing thing isn't that someone is going to be damned; the amazing thing is that someone is going to be saved. And even more amazing is that God has told us that He wills, He desires, He wishes that *everyone* would be saved. And then He gives us the means—money, time, language, writing, printing, television, radio—every possible means of communication. He has put all these things at our disposal in order to bring His life-giving, saving Word to the world. That is what He wants. That is why we preach the Gospel, the Good News, and why we are praying and working to reach more and more people.

Because God says He wants "all men to be saved" (1 Tim. 2:4), He has offered them the gift of His Son, Jesus Christ. You don't have to be damned! You can be saved! Jesus Christ is the Lord and Savior of the world, and through His suffering and death, your sins have been taken away. If you believe in Him, you will be saved! Through His Word, God sends the Holy Spirit into your heart, giving you the gift of faith. You will then know Jesus Christ as your personal Savior and Lord.

The next time some people say how loving they are, accept that tongue-in-cheek, because quite frankly, they don't know what they're talking about. Only God is *true* love, and He has given us a Savior in His Son, Jesus Christ.

Where are you in your relationship with God? Do you see Him as a loving God who has sent you a Savior? Do you know His Son, Jesus Christ? Are *you* saved?

11

Risen

It's wonderful to know that there is resurrection from the dead and life eternal. First Corinthians 15 deals with the subject of resurrection. Chapter 15 is just loaded with resurrection theology. It fills our minds with the importance of its message. It's another one of the key chapters of the Bible.

> *1 Cor. 15:1–2:* And now I want to remind you, my brothers, of the Good News which I preached to you, which you received, and on which your faith stands firm. That is the gospel, the message that I preached to you. You are saved by the gospel if you hold firmly to it—unless it was for nothing that you believed (TEV).

St. Paul says our entire faith is based upon the foundation that Jesus Christ rose from the dead. It is that Good News that saves those who firmly believe it.

> *1 Cor. 15:3–4:* I passed on to you what I received, which is of the greatest importance: that Christ died for our sins, as written in the Scriptures; that He was buried and that He was raised to life three days later, as written in the Scriptures (TEV).

Those two verses summarize our Christian faith. The fact that Jesus suffered and died for our sins, was buried, and then rose again to be our Lord and Savior. There you have it.

What follows in verses 5 through 8 are the accounts of Jesus' appearances to various people after His resurrection.

He appeared to Peter, to the 12 apostles, to more than 500 of His followers, to James, and to Paul himself.

> *1 Cor. 15:9–10:* For I am the least of all the apostles—I do not even deserve to be called an apostle, because I persecuted God's church. But by God's grace I am what I am, and the grace that He gave me was not without effect. On the contrary, I have worked harder than any of the other apostles, although it was not really my own doing, but God's grace working with me (TEV).

It seems to me that if we capture this confession of St. Paul we'll have a very good way of explaining the growth in our Christian lives. God expects us to make progress. He wants us to be more obedient and to do good works. All the way through the New Testament Jesus speaks of the growth and maturity He expects to see in us. But here we see the insight St. Paul had discovered. He realized that he was not doing these things, but it was Christ living in him. It was His kindness and His grace that was working upon Paul and helping him make progress.

> *1 Cor. 15:12:* Now since our message is that Christ has been raised from death, how can some of you say that the dead will not be raised to life? (TEV).

Paul is saying that those people miss the point. They fail to understand that if there is no resurrection of the dead, then Christ must still be dead. But the fact is that Christ did actually rise from the dead and has become the first of millions who will come back to life again some day.

> *1 Cor. 15:21–22:* For just as death came by means of a man, in the same way the rising from death comes by means of a man. For just as all people die because of their union with Adam, in the same way all will be raised to life because of their union with Christ (TEV).

Through Adam all people fell into sin, and it became the natural state of every human being. Through Christ we have all been forgiven, if we believe in Him as our personal Savior.

Christ has risen from the dead and defeated Satan. Those of us who believe in Him as our personal Savior shall also rise from the dead and live eternally with Him in heaven. Our last enemy—death—has been conquered. That's the beautiful news of Christ's resurrection.

12

Scapegoat

There are many beautiful names for Jesus, our Lord. He is the Christ, the Messiah, Immanuel. He is the Way, the Truth, and the Life. He is the Good Shepherd. He is also the Lamb of God. He is the Light of the World and King of Kings. There are many other beautiful names that define and describe His work, such as Savior, Redeemer, Lord. Each of these names has a beauty of its own, but one that stands out in an unusual way is found in Leviticus 16. Actually, Christ is not called by the name specifically, but the entire chapter leads us to understand that Christ is our *scapegoat*.

Have you noticed that although we generally agree that we are sinful and that none of us is perfect, we find it difficult when the guilt begins to zero in on us *individually*? As long as we are talking corporately, or as a nation, or as a church body, or as a family, we feel somewhat safe in confessing our sins because *we are not alone.* But when an accuser confronts us individually with a specific sin, we begin to squirm and feel uncomfortable. Now the spotlight is upon us. The difficulty, of course, is that it is painful to repent. It is much easier for us to *explain* our sins and *excuse* them than to confess them. The need to confess them requires humility—and the human being does not find himself or herself naturally humble.

The first two people created found that they also had the tendency to blame their sins on others. As we push our guilt upon others (transference), we are attempting to squirm out of owning up to our personal guilt. When Adam and Eve fell into sin, they were immediately aware that something had changed. God, who had been on a friendly, personal basis with them, now seemed to be alienated because they felt different. They knew something had changed. They felt fear and they felt shame. When God came and called for them, they ran and hid in the bushes. In a vain attempt to hide their shame, they made clothing from leaves.

When God spoke with them about their problem, Adam, instead of repenting, used Eve as his "scapegoat." In effect, he said, "God, it's all the fault of the woman you gave me." In fact, Adam's reply could almost indicate that he was actually blaming God. After all, it was God who had given him the woman. In effect, Adam was saying, "It's not my fault. I didn't put her here. You're really responsible, God. Don't blame me."

Then, as the spotlight turned on Eve, we see that she too refused to accept the blame and immediately tried to find another "scapegoat." She, in a sense, also blamed God. She said, "It's all the fault of the snake." The implication was clear. She didn't create the snake, and she didn't want to be responsible for the fact that the snake tricked her.

It has been going on ever since. Humanity is constantly refusing to accept its own guilt and is always looking for a "scapegoat." In Leviticus 16, we see a reference to the Day of Atonement, a festival celebrated by the children of Israel once a year. One portion of it deals with two goats. As we see in Lev. 16:4, the first goat was slaughtered and its blood was sprinkled as a symbolic purifier. It should be obvious that the goat itself was innocent, yet its blood became the symbol of forgiveness for the children of Israel.

But there was a second goat. In verse 20, we read that Aaron was told to symbolically place his hands upon the head of the second goat. In so doing, he was to transfer all of the sins of Israel upon the goat. After this was done, a special person took the goat out into the middle of a barren wilderness and left it there to wander off and forever be lost and forgotten. The symbol was clear. The sins of the people now were to be forgotten and totally removed—never more to return.

In this way, these two goats became types or symbols of what our Lord and Savior was going to do for us by His suffering and death. We are told in the Scriptures that it is im-

49

possible to hide from our sins and we cannot escape the judgment of God. He knows our very thoughts. There are no secrets from God. So it is foolish to attempt to push our sins off on someone else. We are, in fact, hopeless before a righteous God. There seems to be no way out.

Then comes the good news! There is a scapegoat! Jesus Christ becomes our Scapegoat. Our sins are placed upon Him. That's incredible! But that is precisely what God says. He sent His Son, Jesus Christ, to this earth in order to take our place— and in so doing, He has carried our sins Himself upon the cross. Through His death, we have been forgiven. His innocent blood was shed for the guilty. As incredible as it must have seemed to the people of Israel that their sins could be forgiven by the blood of an innocent goat, so also it seems incredible to some people that their sins can be washed away by the blood of Jesus Christ. Yet, that is God's promise! Through the death of His Son, we are forgiven, if we trust and believe in Him as our personal Savior.

As our scapegoat, Jesus has taken our sins and removed them from us. They are forever forgotten, and they are no longer before the face of our Father in heaven. They are removed as far as the East is from the West. They need no longer haunt us, and there is no possibility that they can harm us anymore. When Christ forgives sin, He also takes away the guilt. We are new creatures. We have a new life in Jesus Christ. And by the power of His Holy Spirit, we can be renewed and live a life with joy and with a daily assurance of Christ's forgiveness and love.

We are never told whether one of the Israelite scapegoats ever accidently wandered back from the wilderness. I know of no record of such a goat suddenly turning up in one of the villages in the desert, but it may have happened. One thing is certain. There need be no fear of some accidental ineffectiveness of our Scapegoat—Jesus Christ. He has removed our sins forever. His forgiveness is definite and final. If you believe in Him, you will have eternal life. And if you come clothed in His blood, before the throne of the Father, you will be assured of eternal salvation. With this in mind, read Isaiah 53.

13

Thanks

By nature we are *not* grateful. "Thanking" does not come naturally to us. In fact, by nature we are self-serving and greedy. Our human nature finds it impossible to comprehend that "it is more blessed to give than to receive." We are quite willing to provide a *want list* for those who plan to shop for a gift. Hardly ever do we try to avoid someone who offers to help us or give us something. We really do like to *get*—that's part of our sinful nature. Because of such self-centeredness, we have difficulty remembering to be thankful. In fact, at times we find it easier to murmur and complain than to give thanks.

The mature Christian should be different! We should grow to understand and remember that all good gifts come from God. We should daily practice giving thanks until it becomes a regular part of our lives. It will require discipline and training just like any other spiritual gift.

I am thankful for the most priceless gift of all (totally beyond comprehension)—that God has given us His Son as our Savior. What an overwhelming gift! (2 Cor. 9:15).

I am thankful for the freedom that I have in Christ! To be free from sin also means to be free from my guilt. I am no longer a slave to sin. I can choose to live for Christ. Even the daily burdens of life can be turned over to Him. He will care for me. To know Christ is to be really free! (Read Gal. 5:1 and Rom. 6:17–18.)

I am thankful for the certainty of my final victory! There is no doubt that I will spend eternity with God. My certainty does not come from myself, but is based entirely on God's promise to me. He has made me His own child. He promises me that no one or no thing can pluck me from His hand. (The possibility of "falling away" exists if anyone becomes careless with their spiritual life. That is not God's fault.) God's Spirit will daily renew and strengthen those who seek Him. Through God's Word and the magnificent meal of His body and blood, He will keep me in His eternal grasp—and I will live with Him forever. I thank God for that! (1 Cor. 15:57).

14

The Gift

In most families there is usually a joker who wraps Christmas presents in a surprising way. These jokers usually start with an oversized box. When the receiver of the gift opens this outer box, he or she discovers that it is merely filled with paper and another smaller box. As the smaller box is opened, it contains yet a smaller size box. And so it goes on and on until the treasured gift is finally found.

Christmas is the time when we remember God's greatest gift to mankind—His son, Jesus Christ. For many, this valuable gift may have been overlooked because of all the empty boxes and "trimmings" with which the world surrounds the Christmas season.

The "trimmings" of Christmas are not necessarily evil in themselves. But if they detract from the real meaning of Christmas and keep someone from seeing Jesus, then they become evil.

Think of the noise and celebration of past Christmases. It's easy to get swept up in all of the confusion and commotion. Some people even get in a frenzy over spending money. Certainly our materialistic world encourages the tradition of giving and receiving gifts. A person could get totally "wrapped up" in this outer layer of "trimmings" and actually miss the real meaning of Christmas.

Then you have the emotional highs of the season. A lot of people travel to visit relatives. It's family reunion time. The emotions are on the surface. Memories go back to past years and past relationships. Familiar music rings in our ears. People can become very involved in the emotional "trimmings" of the season. That's okay. But, if that's all that happens, they have really missed *the gift*.

You must cut through all the trimmings and see Jesus Christ as your personal savior. When the Holy Spirit enables you to see and acknowledge Him as the Lord of your life and your personal Savior who has freed you from your sins and given you life eternal, then you have found the real meaning and *the gift* of Christmas.

But some people refuse the gift. Some cannot believe that they have been freed from sin and from its guilt. Others think that it can't be so easy and therefore refuse to believe that Jesus is *their* Savior. It is really an either/or situation. You cannot be indifferent about Jesus.

In Matthew 27 we read the account of Jesus as He was brought before Pilate. Pilate tried desperately to rid himself of the decision he faced. First he asked all kinds of questions. Then he put the decision to the crowd, assuming they would certainly call for Jesus' release. Instead they chose Barabbas. We follow that account all the way through chapter 27, and we see that Jesus, after being mocked and ridiculed, is finally condemned to death. And then we read the account of the crucifixion itself.

Who do you say Jesus is? Ultimately, Pilate was unable to avoid the confrontation with Jesus Christ, just as anyone living today who has heard His message and His claim to be the Son of God has to make a choice. Either Jesus is who He claims to be—the very Son of God—or He is the worst imposter and most deceitful person who ever lived. He is one or the other, and you have to make up your mind.

There are still people today who try to get around that issue. Just as Pilate washed his hands thinking he could absolve himself, people today try to compromise. They say, "Jesus certainly was a wonderful person ... He was one of the greatest and most influential leaders the world has ever known ... His teachings are quite good ... " They are in favor of the majority of what Jesus taught and said. Some will even go so far as to say, "He was a savior of the people," comparing Him to other leaders who have suffered for their people. He gave them a goal, gave them purpose and reason to live, lifted them up from earthly problems, and pointed them toward spiritual thinking.

But you can say all those things and believe all those things and *not* be saved! "Believing" in that way is *not* a confession of faith. It is merely saying that Jesus Christ is a man who is godlike, or a god who is manlike. In either case, it misses the teaching of the Holy Scriptures. The Scriptures say: (1) That Jesus is true God, and (2) that He existed with the Father and the Holy Spirit before the world was made, and (3) that the Triune God—the one and only true God—is in the person of the Father, Son, and Holy Spirit.

It is Jesus, the Son—second person of that Trinity—whom the Father sent to this earth as a human being (the entire point of the Christmas celebration) to be born of the Virgin Mary. He, true God, came to earth, taking on the form of a man. And Jesus Christ, as true God and true man, went to the cross, suffered in our place, and fulfilled the payment of our sins. And being resurrected from the dead, the Father accepted His death in our place. He ascended back to His throne in heaven to be at the right hand of His Father.

The promise of the Scriptures is that this Jesus, true God, is going to return again. He will come, not in humility, but in all His power and glory. He will not come as a helpless infant in a manger, but as the resurrected Lord and ruler over all things in heaven and earth. He will come to His throne surrounded by the heavenly hosts in all His majesty. This Jesus Christ, the Lord God Almighty, the personal Savior of everyone who believes in Him, will rule and reign over all things.

When God the Holy Spirit converts us, He also changes our will so that we can think positively in terms of His will for us, as we consider these questions:

Do you believe in Jesus Christ as your personal Lord and Savior?

Do you accept the forgiveness that He offers you?

Do you daily live your life in a consistent walk with Him, asking for His presence and direction, waiting in sincere anticipation for His return, and knowing and believing that He could return at any moment?

I believe that we need to:

- Confess our faith with every other Christian all around the world.
- Become more obedient to God's Word.
- Be more zealous in proclaiming that Word.
- Eagerly anticipate His return.

Jesus is God's true Son. He is the Savior of the world. To everyone who accepts Him and confesses Him and believes in Him, He will give eternal life.

I ask you today to boldly and proudly confess your faith. Join hands in fellowship with other believers in Jesus Christ. Pray and worship more committedly. And under God's blessings, confess Him before the world as your Lord and Savior.

Jesus—There is no other name under heaven whereby men can be saved (Acts 4:12). May Jesus be with you always.

15

God's Love

Love. What an exciting word! The Scriptures tell us over and over again about God's love, and yet there is one particular verse that summarizes it more beautifully than any other. That verse is John 3:16, a favorite of practically every child of God. It is one of the best known and most memorized verses in the Bible. In this one tiny verse we see the entire message of God's love for the world.

> *John 3:16:* For God so loved the world that He gave His only Son, that whoever believes in Him should not perish but have eternal life.

The source of our love is God. If it were not for God's action, man would be hopelessly lost. There is no way we can take away our own sins. So it has to be God who initiates the action, and this verse spells that out. God is the source of our salvation.

The love of God is astounding and beyond comprehension. We read in the Scriptures references to the wrath of God, the judgment of God. We can understand why God would be upset with us when we recognize our rebellion, our habitual sins, and our unwillingness to follow Him. We deserve His wrath and judgment. But instead He offers us love!

Love is a basic need we all have from childhood. We need to have the feeling that we are acceptable and that we are loved. Now God Himself comes to us and says, "I love you." This isn't the fickle kind of love that will remain only a short while and then leave. His love for us is so compelling, so overwhelming, so great, that He gave His only Son for us!

Jesus took our place upon the cross to suffer our punishment, to die in our place so that we need not die eternally. Now we can have life through Him. That's the overwhelming love of God! And He gives and offers this love to the entire world!

Let's suppose a person has a birthday present for you and says, "This gift is yours." Then you would know that it is *specifically* for you. You didn't earn it. You didn't buy it. But it is freely given to you. Now, suppose you say, "No thanks, I don't want the gift. I won't accept it." Then, obviously, you will not benefit from the gift.

God offers us a gift—His son Jesus Christ. He died once for all the sins of the entire world. All those who have ever lived or who will ever live have their sins forgiven in the suffering, death, and resurrection of Jesus Christ. But how does that become *your* personal gift? That comes about through *faith*. Through His Word, God sends His Holy Spirit into your life and converts you. He miraculously changes you from a rebellious sinner to a child of God—believing and accepting His gift of His son, Jesus Christ.

If that faith has not been placed in your heart, and if you do not trust in Jesus Christ as your personal Savior, then the benefits and blessings of Christ's suffering and death are not yet yours personally. But they can be. God invites you to be His own child and have that gift of salvation and eternal life.

John 3:16 contains a warning to those who refuse God's gift. "... whoever believes in Him should not perish ..." This also means that those who *do not* believe in Jesus *will* perish. In John 14:6 we read that Jesus said: "I am the way, and the truth, and the life; no one comes to the Father, but by me." The Scriptures are very definite about this. There is a judgment. God is righteous.

So in these verses we are given a warning—a warning that is repeated throughout Scripture: Those who do not believe in Jesus Christ cannot have eternal salvation. But those who believe in Jesus Christ, personally trust Him for their salvation, and rely on Him as their personal Savior, will not perish, but will have eternal life. We have been given a Savior. We need not perish. We will have eternity with God.

This eternal life, we are told, is free from all sin. That is why there will be no death. Death is a part of our sinful world just like weariness, grief, sorrow, pain, and sickness. All of these things will be absent from heaven. There will be no sins committed in heaven, and as a result, none of the consequences of sin will be there either. In heaven we will experience a life that will be free from all pain, all sorrow, all despair and weariness, and everything else that is negative. Instead, we will be filled with the glory of God. We will be before His throne rejoicing and celebrating.

PART 2

Coping: Our Relationship with Ourself

(Personal)

16

Forward!

There are times in our lives when we come up against what seems to be a brick wall. There doesn't seem to be anywhere to go. There doesn't seem to be any solution to our problems. There doesn't seem to be any hope. I've felt that way at times in my life.

If you have done any living at all, chances are you have had moments when everything seems to cave in. At those times we say trouble comes in bunches. Maybe some of you are in a time of despair right now. Perhaps three or four things have gone wrong simultaneously. Trouble can come in torrents, and we feel that we cannot move forward.

It is my joy and privilege as a spokesman for the true triune God—Father, Son, and Holy Spirit—to tell you there is hope. If you are in a situation where you feel you can't take another step, move forward! Move forward with the knowledge that God is with you, and He will work it out and take care of you.

I want to refer you to a text in the Old Testament where I received this thought I'm sharing with you. It is a familiar one in Exodus 14. In verse 15 we read this question and incredible command from God to Moses: "Why are you crying for help? Tell the people to move forward."

Let's review Exodus so we can understand what an incredible command that was. The people of Israel had been held captive by the Egyptians and had worked in slavery there for many, many years. Then God sent Moses and Aaron to lead the people out of captivity. Remember how they began negotiations with Pharaoh for the release of the Israelites? Each time Pharaoh said, "No, I will not let the people of Israel go." Well, finally through Moses and Aaron, God sent ten plagues upon the Egyptians. The tenth one was death to every first born Egyptian son, including Pharaoh's. That finally brought Pharaoh to his knees begging for mercy and saying, "Okay. All right. Your people can go." Then Moses and Aaron began to lead the people across the wilderness toward the Promised Land.

But it didn't take long for Pharaoh to change his mind. He realized he was losing hundreds of thousands of slaves. He decided to send his army to bring them back.

Now the Israelites had gone some distance, and God directed them to take a turn so that at the time they saw the army of Pharaoh pursuing them, they were right on the banks of the Red Sea. Where could they go? Here came the trained soldiers of the Egyptian army. The Israelites had no weapons and were not trained to fight. It seemed like a hopeless situation. The army was behind them and the sea was in front of them.

They began to pray to God. There was also a lot of murmuring and complaining to Moses because of the hopeless mess he had gotten them into. Then God came to them and said to Moses, "Tell the people to move forward. Lift up your walking stick and hold it out over the sea. The water will divide and the Israelites will be able to walk through the sea on dry ground."

Miraculously the Red Sea parted, and the Israelites safely crossed to the other side. Then the Egyptians started across. In Ex. 14:26 we read that God said to Moses, "Hold out your hand over the sea, and the water will come back over the Egyptians and their chariots and drivers"(TEV).

Obviously, God could have parted the water and brought it back without Moses. God does not have to use people. But He chooses to use people. Many, many times He chose to use Moses.

In the same way, God will choose to send someone into your life to help you in your time of need. Maybe it is someone who is already there. In some way God will use people, empower them, give them strength, knowledge, ability, whatever is necessary in that circumstance to help you. Just trust God.

Many times God will miraculously deliver you, just as He did the Israelites. I am convinced that miracles still happen. God is constantly at work in our lives and when He chooses, miracles happen.

One thing is certain. When God says to move forward in your life, that is exactly what He wants you to do. Move forward with total confidence that He is with you and will take care of you.

17

Salvation

"Salvation" is a beautiful word for every child of God. We need to think about our salvation and make certain that we are giving it the full attention it really deserves.

Obviously, the most important part of salvation is the realization that we have life eternal through our Lord and Savior, Jesus Christ. All who believe that Jesus Christ is their personal Savior and trust in Him to forgive their sins have salvation. In the Scriptures we find many references to this. One that isn't discussed enough is in Titus 2:11–14:

> For the grace of God has appeared for the salvation of all men, training us to renounce irreligion and worldly passions, and to live sober, upright, and godly lives in this world, awaiting our blessed hope, the appearing of the glory of our great God and Savior Jesus Christ, who gave Himself for us to redeem us from all iniquity and to purify for Himself a people of His own who are zealous for good deeds.

The most familiar aspect of salvation is the salvation of our souls. And we know there are only two options: either eternity in hell, if repentance is not present and salvation is rejected; or eternity in heaven if, through the Holy Spirit, Jesus Christ is accepted as our personal Savior and we believe in Him for the forgiveness of our sins. I believe most people realize that "everlastingness" is a big, big aspect of what salvation is all about.

So we speak of the salvation of the soul. But we need to speak about other things, too, in connection with salvation.

We need to give it the full meaning it deserves. For instance, our *bodies* will also be saved. The Christian faith is the only religion in the world that teaches that the body was created by God and that it is good. Christians believe their bodies will be resurrected from the dead and spend eternity with the soul in heaven. In many religions the body is looked upon as a handicap to the spirit. Some teach that the body must somehow be disposed of and discarded. All such teachings are incorrect and contrary to God's Word. The Bible teaches that the body, as God created it, was perfect and good. It is sin that has brought harm and imperfection to the body. It is because of sin that we have disease, illness, maladies, and handicaps. It is because of sin that we die.

The resurrected body will be renewed and glorified. It will be perfect because all sin will be gone. On Judgment Day the resurrected body will have no sin. That means the aging process, for instance, will be gone. It means the aches and pains and weariness will be gone because those are the symptoms and the results of sin. So when the Christian speaks of salvation, it's not merely the soul (although that is a great part of it, as we mentioned earlier), but it is also the body. God will restore us as total persons, not just a part of us. If we believe in Jesus Christ as our personal Savior, we will be with God—body and soul—in heaven.

But St. Paul, as he was writing to Titus, took the meaning of salvation a step further. He said that we should realize that salvation is not merely something out in the distant future, it is not merely something that relates to our life after death, but it is something that we ought to be aware of right now and consciously realize that it should be affecting our lives today. Yes, right now while we are alive, right here on earth.

I believe it is that aspect of salvation that the church also needs to bring to the attention of its members. To begin with, it has to do with the conduct of our lives. To reiterate St. Paul's words, "... training us to renounce irreligion and worldly passions, and to live sober, upright, and godly lives *in this world....*" And that's the point. Salvation, by the grace of God, if it is genuine and true, will change our way of living and give us a new hope! We are waiting for the appearance of our Lord, Jesus Christ! Our desire is to be His people, eager to do His will. This is essential for the Christian church to hear, to believe, to practice. Our lives are to be controlled and guided by the power of God.

This salvation which we have received through God's own Son, Jesus Christ, is not only something that *we look forward to*, it is also something *we already have*. Our lives and our conduct here on earth are going to indicate whether or not we genuinely believe that Jesus Christ is our personal Savior.

This salvation, this new birth, comes in many ways. It also comes at various "speeds" in the hearts and lives of people. For instance, the conversion of St. Paul (Acts 9) was very sudden and miraculous—it took place within the course of a couple of seconds. God can still do that and at times chooses to. But generally speaking, it is a slower process. It often takes the witness of numerous people.

We know that some in the Bible, like Lydia (Acts 16:11–15), were converted at the preaching of a message of God's Word. Others, perhaps, may come to faith in a more gradual way as small changes take place in their lives. They become convinced of sin and realize that they need help. But maybe they have not yet really opened their heart to God. God is willing and desirous to have them become His children. He is calling them and inviting them to accept Jesus Christ as their personal Lord and Savior.

I believe that every time the Word of God is preached and proclaimed, He is calling people to repentance and salvation. Those of you who are not yet committed to Jesus Christ, please hear the invitation. We want you to know that God loves *you*. He knows you personally. He loves you personally. He wants you personally.

Today, as you read these words based on God's Holy Scripture, I invite you in the name of our Lord and Savior, Jesus Christ, to turn to Him. Repent of your sins. Ask Him to give you the joy of eternal salvation. That salvation will not only change your future eternally, but it will also change your life now! God is powerful, so don't doubt Him. He will send His Holy Spirit upon you, and you will have the *gift of salvation*— today and forever!

18

Goals

It's not too surprising that one of the prescriptions for people who are emotionally ill is to set goals for their lives. Everyone needs to have a sense of direction, a feeling of accomplishment, a goal, a purpose—some priority.

A beautiful text that suggests this thought is found in Philippians 3. I want to apply it to this goal: *Finding our life's purpose centered in Jesus Christ!* That's the major point of this text. I want to apply it also to the need for setting goals in our daily life. We should have spiritual goals, physical goals, emotional goals, psychological goals, and mental goals.

Let's begin by reading Phil. 3:8–14.

> Indeed I count everything as loss because of the surpassing worth of knowing Christ Jesus my Lord. For His sake I have suffered the loss of all things, and count them as refuse, in order that I may gain Christ and be found in Him, not having a righteousness of my own, based on law, but that which is through faith in Christ, the righteousness from God that depends on faith; that I may know Him and the power of His resurrection, and may share His sufferings, becoming like Him in His death, that if possible I may attain the resurrection from the dead.
>
> Not that I have already obtained this or am already perfect; but I press on to make it my own, because Christ Jesus has made me His own. Brethren, I do not consider that I have made it my own; but one thing I do, forgetting what lies

behind and straining forward to what lies ahead,
I press on toward the goal for the prize of the
upward call of God in Christ Jesus.

You can see in these words the urgency in the mind of
St. Paul. Many times when I have read this text I have thought
that there was a great deal of comfort in these words, "forgetting what lies behind." There is comfort, in one sense, in
that all past sins have been forgiven by Jesus, and the past
cannot haunt us nor in any way ruin our lives. Today is a new
day. And under Christ's resurrection power that Paul speaks
of here, we have an opportunity to glorify His name in all
that we do and say. So the past does not control us. We strive
and look forward to the future.

But there is another way to understand this text. In the
life of Paul we get a little clue of what may be going on in
his mind here. Paul must have been a very gutsy, energetic,
and diligent person. We can tell that from his writings and
also by what we know about his life historically. Now, he no
doubt felt that he was about as good as anyone around. You
remember even in one of his epistles he said if he was to be
measured by his own righteousness, by what he did (and, of
course, Paul clearly knew that he was *not* going to be measured by that) he felt he had done pretty well (Phil. 3:4–6).

What Paul is saying is that it doesn't matter even if you've
been very, very good and done a thousand good things, you
can't display these and say, "Boy, do I ever deserve something
from God! Boy have I *earned* something!" Paul says that just
doesn't hold water because he has discovered his righteousness is not in what he has done, but his righteousness is in
what God has done through His Son, Jesus Christ.

As you read those opening words of Phil. 3:8, you will
see that Paul repeats that thought over and over again, making
it clear that the only reason he feels he can come into the
presence of God is that he has been "made right" with God
through Jesus Christ. Now Paul is growing. He says he has
learned how to share his sufferings. He has also learned how
to understand the importance of Christ. He has learned, in
that opening sentence of this text, that everything else is just

like refuse or garbage because of the one surpassing thing, and that is *knowing Jesus Christ*. That is the only thing that counts in life! Everything else by comparison is worthless. And, having learned this, he presses on toward the goal. Now the goal ultimately is to know Jesus Christ and live for Him and to glorify His name.

But what are the intermediate or short-term goals? For a goal to be a real goal it has to be measurable. There has to be a time element in it so that you can see whether or not you've met it. For instance, to glorify God is a beautiful purpose, but to make that into a goal you have to get specific and say, "I'll worship God every Sunday this month." Now you've made it into a *specific goal* that is measurable. You'll know whether or not you have met the goal at the end of the month.

Or perhaps you say, "I'm going to be more patient." That is a beautiful *purpose*. But to get *specific* and make it a *goal*, you would have to say something like this, "I will not lose my temper with my children at any time this week." Now, you see, you have made it specific and measurable. You've set a time element to it, and it's a specific goal.

If you were to say, "I will give more to the Lord," that is also a beautiful purpose. But to make it a specific goal you would have to say, "I will increase my giving by five dollars a week for the next six months."

Or if you say something like, "I'll witness more for my Lord," to make it measurable you would have to say, "I'll speak to my neighbor before the week is over."

What I'm urging you to do is to strive toward a *specific goal* to glorify God. I believe that many people live their lives without really accomplishing a great deal because they don't set specific goals.

I'm urging you to get that mood that St. Paul had and realize that God has "put His hand" on you. He has called you and chosen you! Now He didn't do that just for the fun of it. He did that so you would work for Him, glorify Him, and praise His holy name. God expects you to do great things to the honor of His name.

In order to accomplish that, it seems as though He has

designed us to set goals. I like the way Paul says he is moving toward that goal. He doesn't say, "I'm rambling toward the goal," and he doesn't say, "I will casually lope toward the goal." He says, "I will *strain*, I am *pressing* on toward the goal." Now to get specific. What are you going to do *today* to honor God? Are you going to talk to someone about Him? Are you going to increase your prayer life? Are you going to increase your giving? Are you going to increase your patience and love? What are you specifically going to do to glorify God in your life *today*?

Friends in Christ, make a specific goal to glorify God in your life and press on, strive diligently to worship Him and serve Him in your life!

19

Thorn

Thorn as in the statement of St. Paul, ". . . a *thorn* in the flesh."
Let's read 2 Cor. 12:7–9 where that phrase comes from:

> And to keep me from being too elated by the
> abundance of revelations, a thorn was given me
> in the flesh, a messenger of Satan, to harass me,
> to keep me from being too elated. Three times
> I besought the Lord about this, that it should
> leave me; but He said to me, "My grace is suffi-
> cient for you, for my power is made perfect in
> weakness." I will all the more gladly boast of my
> weaknesses, that the power of Christ may rest
> upon me.

I suppose each of us, at one time or another, has had a
thorn in the flesh. Maybe right now you are dealing with a
thorn in the flesh—something that you already have come to
God about numerous times, but it still hangs on, and in your
opinion, is destroying your life. We all have times when we
feel like that.

Let's look at what some of these thorns in the flesh could
be in our lives. Have there been times when you've felt like
a failure? Maybe you feel that way now. Or maybe in your
life at this moment the thorn in the flesh is disappointment.
One of the saddest thorns is poor health.

Maybe your thorn is persecution. The Bible talks a lot
about persecution—people who were ridiculed, oppressed,
taunted, and even killed because of their faith. Somewhere in
the world today people are being persecuted because of their
love for Jesus Christ.

Or maybe your particular problem right now is the loss of a loved one, and you are saying, "This is really tough to take. I don't think life is being very fair at the moment. I'm in despair. I'm lonely. I feel as though God has forgotten me."

Well, dear people, life is never simple, and all of life's problems—despair, discouragement, illness, failure, persecution, bereavement—are common to every Christian just as they are to every unbeliever. Everyone in the human race experiences these trials. The difference is that we hold on to Jesus Christs' guarantee and promise to lead us through and to bless us as a result of the problems and difficulties.

Some people have called life's problems the University of Hard Knocks. This is where the edges are taken off, and we get polished up a little bit through the maturity of living.

The process of having our rough edges taken off is similar to cutting a diamond. Certainly at first glance it appears as though the stone is going to be destroyed because a sharp-pointed chisel is cutting it. But then we see that the craftsman knows what he is doing—that he is making a facet to pick up the reflection of light so that it will shine all the more brilliantly.

In the same way, God is molding and shaping us. He knows exactly what He wants us to be. Although He knows what the end product should look like, we sometimes cry out because we do not understand. We feel we are being persecuted, or we feel our disappointments are too intense, or we feel the burden of ill health is too heavy, or our bereavement is overwhelming, and we cry out as if we did not trust God or believe that He knows and sees our situation. I would like to remind you again that we have His word and promise, His explicit, total, loving, complete assurance that He will never leave us, never forsake us, and that He will always remain with us. He will turn every evil to our good, and He will keep His promise! If the University of Hard Knocks has you down, lift up your eyes, look to the Lord, trust in Him, hold onto Him in faith, and He will deliver you! He will, in one way or another, set you free, cause your heart to rejoice, and give you a victory! In His way and time He will lift you up and enable you to withstand. He will bless you!

20

Songs

We know how important moods are in our daily lives. And we know the importance that music plays in affecting our moods. If you are listening to a piece that's very sober and slow, it can put you in a depressed mood. I know that certain types of music—rock, for instance—can irritate because you hear the same sounds over and over again. In the same way, other types of music can uplift you. How can anyone listen to Handel's *Messiah* and the beautiful "Hallelujah Chorus" without being uplifted to the heights of spiritual enjoyment and thrilled by the majesty of the music?

Songs are important in our daily lives. In Rev. 15:3 we read of God's people singing the song of Moses. But before we begin our discussion of Revelation 15, I want to say a few things about this book of the Bible. Revelation is filled with apocalyptic writing and, as such, it is a very difficult book to understand. Many scholars think they have the answers to unlock its meaning and give all sorts of approaches to its interpretation. Quite frankly, if you read 15 authors on this subject, you will end up with 15 different points of view. So I am not among those who suggest you should struggle with Revelation. But there is certainly something there to be learned. There is a blessing promised to those who read it, so we should not ignore it.

In Revelation 15 we read about a sign of what is going to happen in the last days. We read that the bowls of wrath are going to be poured out upon the people of the earth. Now this is a concept that many people have difficulty with. Whenever in the liturgy of the church year we run into a prayer for God's judgment and wrath upon those who are opposed to His will, some people are troubled. They say, "We don't know if that is consistent with a loving God. We don't know if we want to think about God bringing His judgment on people."

Quite frequently those are the same people who would like to do away with hell and say that ultimately there is no eternal punishment. Those who think that way are flat out denying the Scriptures, and they are making salvation a joke. What is salvation *from* if it is not a salvation *from* judgment and hell? You really have to watch out so that you *don't* begin thinking God is just joking about judgment and hell. He isn't playing a game—trying to scare people into believing in Him and on the last day everyone is going to be saved anyway. People who believe that way are *denying* Scripture and are going to have an enormous shock when they see that God's judgment is going to be complete and full and devastating. In Revelation 15 we see that emphasis: God is going to bring His wrath upon those who reject Him and deny Him and have not accepted His Son, Jesus Christ, as their personal Savior.

I referred to a song. I would like to have you connect Revelation 15 to Exodus 15. We see here two elements: (1) God's deliverance of the people who trusted in Him, and (2) God's destruction of those who did not believe in Him and were opposed to His will. God delivered the children of Israel by creating a miraculous way for them to cross the Red Sea. But when the enemy—the Egyptians—tried to follow, the Red Sea closed over them and destroyed them. What was the reaction of God's people after they safely crossed the Red Sea? In Exodus 15, Moses and the Israelites *sing a song*. They rejoice over the way God overthrew the enemy army—the chariots and the soldiers were wiped out in the sea—the right hand of God is powerful—He breaks the enemy to pieces—His majesty and triumph are overwhelming—His anger blazes out against those who do not obey Him. The people are praising God and celebrating their deliverance from their enemies.

We see this same deliverance taking place in Revelation 15—God delivering His people. He will preserve that remnant. To those who remain faithful, He will give a crown of eternal life. So God is freeing that group who believes and confesses and follows and obeys Him. It is as if with His left hand God is wiping out those who oppose Him, but with His right hand He is setting free and delivering those who are faithful to Him. The redeemed, in this vision of John, see that God has kept His word.

It looks at times as though the enemies of God are gaining the upper hand, the Antichrist, the forces of evil, and those opposed to God are going to be victorious. It is going to be so confusing that the elect of God are almost going to be deceived. But to prevent that, Jesus Christ is going to come and deliver them. When they see their deliverance, when they see that God has saved them, they sing a psalm of praise. They "sing the song of Moses" (v. 3) and God's people: *May we rejoice in His power and in His victory and in His miracles for He has delivered us from the hand of the enemy.* We see this same theme in Habakkuk, as well as throughout the Scriptures.

We often murmur and complain when it seems as though everything is going right for the unbeliever. You may have neighbors who blaspheme God and ridicule your faith, and yet everything seems to be going well for them. They get the job promotions. They are doing great financially. They are seemingly doing well socially. And it just looks as though everything is going their way. You may be inclined to say, "I don't know why I should follow God. Look at my neighbors. They disobey God and everything keeps going right for them. We try to obey and everything goes wrong for us."

That kind of thinking can lead us into a pessimistic, negative frame of mind, wondering whether God has forgotten about us or forsaken us, and whether He is actually going to keep His promise to deliver us. Well, the children of Israel did some of that murmuring and complaining too. But what they forgot is that *God always keeps His promises.* God, using Moses and Aaron, delivered them from their enemy and wiped out the enemy.

So also, God says to you and me, "Even though things may not look very promising at the moment, trust in Me! Remember the past and how I delivered you and helped you. Believe in Me now. I will not forsake you! I will deliver you from your enemies." That will be true throughout our life according to God's will and timing. He alone knows best. It will also be true at the very end on Judgment Day! God is going to wipe out and destroy those who are opposed to Him and His will! He will redeem and free and give eternal life to those who are His believers and followers!

Sing a song of praise!

21

Brain

At times our brain, our thinking, seems to turn towards passing judgment on God. We use the brain God has given us to judge whether He is right and whether He is good. That is a frightening misuse of our brain.

I like what C. S. Lewis wrote on this subject. He said that when the brain is worshiped, then our god is very small and certainly false. In other words, we make our brain our god when we act as if our highest goal is the ability to understand something or to think it through. When you worship your own brain—your intelligence, your wisdom, your astuteness—you are really committing idolatry. Think, for instance, about those people who are mentally ill or have an emotional illness. If they worshiped their mental abilities, their "god" would immediately collapse. You see, what Lewis was pointing out is that those who worship their mind are worshiping a false god—not eternal, not unchanging, but subject to disease, error, delusion, and death.

I became interested in the brain when I was studying to be a hospital chaplain during my seminary training. I spent one year at King's County Hospital in Brooklyn, N. Y. At that time it had 2,700 beds and was one of the country's largest hospitals. Many different types of surgery were performed there, and I had the privilege of meeting many doctors. I had many invitations to observe different surgical procedures.

One of the most interesting operations I watched was brain surgery performed by Dr. Fhru. The patient had a blood clot on the brain that had to be removed. The first step, of course, was to remove a section of the skull to gain access to the clot. The white membrane immediately under the skull reminded me of the white inner layer of an orange. As the doctor just barely touched the scalpel to it, it shrank out of the way and the brain was exposed. People have described the appearance of the brain as being similar to jello or jelly. And that's exactly how it looked to me. I could see the tiny blood clot sitting right on top of the brain.

The clot was removed with a machine similar to a vacuum cleaner with a narrow hose that was connected to a very delicate stainless steel instrument. The point was so thin that I could barely see it. As the surgeon touched that tiny tip to the clot it was immediately suctioned off into a specimen jar. That completed the procedure.

After the skull was closed, the patient went to recovery, where he was closely monitored because the removal of a clot can cause different aftereffects. Sometimes there will be no movement on one side of the body or the other, or the speech can be affected depending on the site of the clot. Or the person can fully recover with no problems.

I mention this to illustrate how easily the brain can be altered. Even one tiny blood clot, much, much smaller than your little fingernail, can wipe out the entire activity of the brain.

This fallible thing called a brain can mislead us and make many errors. So how can anyone be so dumb as to base their faith on whether or not there is a God on his or her own mental ability or understanding? The Scriptures are correct when they say, "The fool has said in his heart, 'There is no God'" (Ps. 14:1).

Certainly you would have to be a fool to say that. If you take the mind God has given you and develop it and use it to His glory, it will be a fantastic gift. But if instead, you use it to judge God, it will become a curse, a false god, a false idol.

The mind is a great gift of God. If properly used, it becomes a marvelous tool to worship and praise God. We have been fearfully and wonderfully made. We have a great God!

22

Serving

In the opening verse of his letter to the Philippians, Paul uses a word that needs to be explained. It's the word "bondservant." He says, "Paul and Timothy, bondservants of Christ Jesus." A bondservant was a slave, somebody who was bought and sold. In our culture today we can hardly imagine that. In early cultures (e.g., Greek, Roman), there were thousands of slaves. (Sadly, in our own country's earlier history, slaves were the "property" of wealthy landowners, especially in the South.) Slaves did not determine their own will; they did the will of their master.

Now Paul is purposely using that word here in the Greek to establish the fact that he no longer considered himself to be his own property. He says, "I do not belong to myself. I am a slave. I belong to someone else, and that someone else is my Lord, Jesus Christ. He dictates to me what to do and what to say and where to be." The point is very clear; Paul saw himself as a willing, voluntary slave of Christ. He wanted it known that the Lord of his life, the owner, the one who controlled his life was Christ Jesus.

With that understanding, Paul's letter to the Philippians continues, "Grace to you and peace from God our Father and the Lord Jesus Christ." Then comes a verse that I have frequently thought about because I'm in a parish where the Lord's presence is felt so strongly and so clearly. This love of the people of God as they express it to me and my family has been so outstanding that I literally join St. Paul when he says here, "I thank my God in all my remembrance of you." In other words, "As I think about you in that congregation at Philippi, I am moved to thank and praise God for you because

I know that what is going on in your hearts and lives is pleasing to Him." And in verse 4, "Always in every prayer of mine for you I pray with joy. You have been participating in the Gospel from the first day until now and I am confident that God has begun a good work in you, who has worked in you to bring you to faith, who has made you partners in the Gospel, is going to continue. He'll perfect it. It will grow more and more in you until the day of the Lord Jesus Christ" (vv. 7–11). That's Judgment Day when Christ will return.

You have to keep in mind that Paul is writing this letter from prison. Beginning at verse 12, he refers to this imprisonment. He says, "Logically, you know, people will think, 'What a shame; now he is in prison; now the work that he is trained and called to do isn't being accomplished.'" But he says, "No, that is not true." As a matter of fact, you notice he is witnessing to the praetorian guard, "and (to) the rest" (v. 13). Things are being accomplished to the glory of God. God is going to turn this into a blessing. Paul talks here about the importance of knowing that *wherever you are you have an opportunity to witness*. So, instead of just sitting there saying, "Woe is me, here I am in prison. I can't get out to do my work," he realizes that he has a captive audience. Someone is always there guarding him. One of the guards is always present, so he always has someone to talk to. That guard can't leave or walk away; he has to stay there. And so Paul saw this as an opportunity to witness, and we can just imagine how he must have talked to the guards about what Christ meant to him and how Christ could help them as well (vv. 12–14).

Beginning at verse 15 he says that some itinerant preachers going around the country at that time had ulterior motives "from envy and rivalry." They were going out preaching, but may have kept the offerings for themselves or something of that sort. There was a lot of concern about that sort of thing. And Paul says something here that must have shocked the church. He says, "Don't get too upset about those people because the main thing is that Christ is being preached." In other words, the primary thing is that the Gospel is getting out and people are hearing about Christ.

There are articles in newspapers and magazines today that

claim some radio and TV ministers are only seeking fame and amassing great wealth. Well, if we go by what St. Paul says here to the Philippians, we shouldn't get too upset about that. Obviously, we ought to try to keep it from happening, but the primary question is: "Are they preaching the Gospel? Are they giving the people they are reaching the right, straight Good News about Jesus Christ and His forgiveness?" If the answer is yes, then we shouldn't worry about too much else because God will take care of it. People are going to be saved whenever that Word is preached and proclaimed.

You might want to keep that in mind if you ever worry about the faith of the pastor, baptizing, serving Holy Communion, preaching, or handling other spiritual matters. You may say to yourself, "I wonder if the pastor really has faith?" Well, even if you had a way of knowing that the pastor was an unbeliever, or if you knew that he was grossly sinning, it still would not in any way affect the baptism, communion, or preaching because these have their affect not from the pastor, nor from the faith of the pastor, but from God. God is the One who is working in baptism, communion, and preaching. God is the One who gives faith, not the pastor.

Now I'm not saying that we shouldn't care whether or not pastors believe in what they preach. How terrible it is when we discover a hypocrite or false prophet who is using people or using the church. We ought to rise up against hypocrisy, stamp it out, and get rid of it. But the point I'm making is the same as what Paul is saying in verse 18, "... whether in pretense or in truth, Christ is proclaimed; and in that I rejoice." We are clear about the subject if we realize that God is the One who converts, God is the One who brings to faith, and God is the one who acts in baptism, communion, and preaching.

So with this kind of introduction, Paul is setting the focus and saying ultimately in verse 20, "It doesn't really matter; one thing is important to me. I have one priority, and that is exalting Jesus Christ, whether I do that in life or death. That is my one goal." And he summarizes that in verse 21 by simply saying, "For me, to live is Christ and to die is gain."

He really believed in eternity. He really believed that he

would be with the Lord after death. He really believed what he preached and what he taught. And he wanted the Philippians not to get all upset about the fact that he was in prison or to start wondering what it all meant, but that they should see that God was still in charge.

If you will read all of Paul's letter to the Philippians you will find many beautiful verses that will just bring joy into your heart and offer great spiritual comfort. I hope it will become one of your favorite letters of the Bible. Once you become acquainted with it, you will fall in love with it. Read it through, "sink your teeth into it," and learn from it. Let God use it as a blessing in your life. And then you can say with Paul, "I have one commitment—to serve the Lord. Whether in my life or in my death, I will serve Him."

23

Shunammite

Shunammite. Have you ever heard this word before? It's the name given to a person from the town of Shunem. We read about a Shunammite woman in the Old Testament in 2 Kings 4:8–37. I'm going to give you the historical background of this account a little later. First, let me quote verse 25 where the story begins. "When the man of God (Elisha) saw her coming, he said to Gehazi, his servant, 'Look yonder is the Shunammite; run at once to meet her and say to her, Is it well with you? Is it well with your husband? Is it well with the child?' And she answered, 'It is well.'"

As far as the historical background goes, we find this particular woman coming in and out of the life of the prophet Elisha. In 2 Kings, chapters 2–13 give us quite a bit of detail on the life and ministry of Elisha. We find out about this Shunammite woman when, on occasion, Elisha would come to Shunem and minister and preach there. She noticed something the other townspeople had not. As she observed Elisha, she saw from time to time how weary he was—sort of beaten and worn out. She not only perceived this, but had a desire to do something about it. After consulting her husband, they made a special little room—"a small roof chamber"—in their home just for the prophet. Whenever he was coming through town, he could go there and rest and regain his strength before moving on to a different community. So we see she recognized when help was needed, and had a heart with a desire to be helpful.

But I suppose the most interesting part of the history of this Shunammite woman was her *contentment*. We read that Elisha was so impressed with her noble gesture in making this room available to him that he offered to do something in return. He granted her a favor. He said to her, "Would you have a word spoken on your behalf to the king or to the commander of the army?" No doubt it was an offer for her husband to be in government or to have an office of prestige and importance. I suppose the average reaction would have been to immediately rejoice and say, "Well, now we can really 'step up' in life. We can move to a finer home and wear better clothes. We can socialize with the elite."

We would expect her to jump at the opportunity and be very eager and zealous to get this promotion for her husband. But instead, she gives a totally different answer. To put it into today's words, she said something like this, "No thank you. We would be 'fish out of water' in that elite circle of the government. We will remain with our own people."

In other words, she very humbly declined that offer to elevate her husband to a position of more prestige. Even though they were wealthy (v. 8), she was concerned that they would lose their real happiness if they began to pursue something that was above and beyond them. So she displays her *contentment*. What a remarkable gift to be content and happy *where you are*. It's a fact: People who are always "social climbing" and striving for more and more *are never satisfied*. They are usually miserable and unhappy as they forfeit today's joys and contentments for tomorrow's "pot of gold." So we see the remarkable contrast in this woman who is *content*, and therefore happy.

Elisha goes a step further and says, "I see you have no son, so I'm going to give you God's promise that you will have a child by this time next year." We see that this miracle was granted to her.

As you follow this story, you'll notice that the boy grew up and on a certain day went into the fields to harvest along with his father and perhaps other neighbors. Suddenly (v. 19), he yelled, "My head! My head!" We don't know exactly whether it was heat stroke or some other problem or disease (the Scriptures don't tell us). But it was obvious that he was *very ill*. His father immediately sent him home. We are told that he was cradled in the arms of his mother and there he died at noon.

Can you imagine the traumatic experience in the life of this Shunammite woman? She had been given a son, a direct blessing from God. Now this son had suddenly become ill and died. It was almost too much for her to bear. We are told that she took the young man's corpse to the room which had been built for the prophet. She placed the dead child on Elisha's bed. Then she told her husband she was going to find Elisha. Her husband wasn't too impressed. He more or less said, "Let's be realistic. The boy is dead, and it's too late." But she insisted on going to tell Elisha what happened.

She found Elisha on Mount Carmel (v. 25). Gehazi, his servant, was with him. Elisha, from the side of the mountain, saw the Shunammite woman coming across the field. He sent Gehazi to meet her and told him to ask her three questions. "Is it well with you? Is it well with your husband? Is it well with your child?"

Gehazi asked the three questions. Now, remember the tragedy the woman just experienced. Listen to her response. She simply said, "It is well."

How remarkable! With her son lying dead and her life shattered, yet she is able to say, "It is well."

I believe we can see many noble characteristics in this Shunammite woman. Even though she passes on the scene only briefly in this account in 2 Kings, we can learn so much from her: her perceptiveness when help was needed; her response and immediate willingness to help; her contentment with what God had given her; and, above all, her faith.

In the midst of trouble and grief, she could still say, "It is well," and be satisfied knowing that somehow God would work things out. And God did grant her a very special blessing through the prophet Elisha. *Her son was brought back to life.* Read that thrilling account in verses 25–37.

We can learn from this Shunammite woman how to become more committed to God. Often, when things go wrong, we mumble and complain and look for all sorts of reasons to justify why these things should not be happening to us. Yet, in this woman we see an example of willingness to *accept* whatever comes her way. She makes the best of it. Even though it looked desperate and hopeless, her faith was there! She believed God could work it out. We know God will work things out for good because He did not spare His own Son for our welfare. Loving us to that degree, He certainly will take care of the rest.

I suspect that of all the women mentioned in the Bible, this Shunammite woman is one of the least known. You may never have heard of her until now. But I hope that now you know about her, you will want to read the account yourself in 2 Kings.

May God grant that the faith of this woman will be an example to us. So, in the midst of trouble, despair, and even grief, we will be able to say, "It is well."

24

Snapshot

Most couples have photo albums of their wedding and of their children growing up. This is one way to remember the past. It's a way of going back and recalling things the way they were. Because of the pictures that help us recall these events, we're able to recelebrate happy times we've experienced.

I would like you to think about a wedding. There were no snapshots taken at this wedding because it was long before the camera was invented. I'm talking about an ancient wedding that took place in the time of Christ and is described in John 2:1–11. We are not told who the couple was. We do know they were married in a little town called Cana. It is up near the Sea of Galilee, which is why it is called "Cana of Galilee." It is still called that today. There is an interesting little red-domed church there which marks the traditional spot where this miracle took place. Jesus had been in the area of Jerusalem where He had just been baptized by John the Baptist. He and His disciples turned around and made the long journey by foot back to Cana in order to attend this wedding.

At the wedding, you recall, there were a number of things taking place. Mary, His mother, came to Jesus to report that the host had run out of wine. This was a rather embarrassing situation. It revealed that the family hadn't planned well, or more people showed up than were expected. Either way, it looked as though things weren't running too smoothly.

Mary tried to get Jesus to intervene and do something. Here is where He reprimanded her. Lovingly, but firmly, Jesus said, "O woman, what have you to do with Me? My hour has not yet come." In other words, *Are you trying to tell Me to do something on your time schedule? Remember, I will determine the time.* When the time was right, Jesus was going to help.

I believe we need to remember this. As we are taking snapshots in our memory of that wedding so long ago, take one of Jesus as He reminds His mother that His time is not yet at hand. Store that mental photograph in your mind because there are going to be times in your life when you are going to feel very strongly that you can tell Jesus what to do and when to do it. There are going to be circumstances in your life when you may come to God and say, "Now, God, I need help. I need it today, and I need it by five o'clock." We would be doing almost exactly what Mary did to Jesus—trying to impose our will over His. But if we reflect upon that, under the gift of the Holy Spirit in faith, we realize how stupid it is.

Now, with your mind, take that little snapshot of that wedding scene at Cana and tuck it away. Hopefully, you will remember not to dictate your timetable and your will to God. Rather, ask of Him, "Lord you determine and decide what is best for me." Carry that snapshot with you spiritually.

Let's take another snapshot. Take a mental picture of those large water pots at the wedding. We are told in verse 6 how many there were (six) and their size (each holding between 20 and 30 gallons). These large pots are filled with water. Now why do I want you to carry this picture around with you? Because I want you to be aware of the fact that Jesus moved into action. He did something. He turned the water into wine. We have to remember that. When we are waiting upon the Lord, we can become impatient and discouraged. We feel God isn't going to help. He isn't going to do anything. And if He does, it will be too late. We despair and lose hope almost like David. He frequently was discouraged as he waited upon the Lord. So remember in this snapshot that Jesus took action.

Isn't it comforting to know that Jesus is concerned! He tells us that He knows all about us:

But now says the Lord ... Fear not, for I have

redeemed you, I have called you by name, you are Mine (Is. 43:1).

... These may forget, yet I will not forget you. Behold I have graven you on the palms of my hands (Is. 49:15–16).

For I know the plans I have for you, says the Lord, plans for welfare and not for evil, to give you a future and a hope (Jer. 29:11).

Are not five sparrows sold for two pennies? And not one of them is forgotten before God. Why, even the hairs of your head are all numbered. Fear not, you are of more value than many sparrows (Luke 12:6–7).

The Lord knows the thoughts of man (Ps. 94:11).

Those are not only wonderful promises, but also very comforting words. We not only have a God who *speaks* of love, but a God who *loves*. When God chooses, He will act. It will always be the right time, and it will always be the right action.

If you recall those water pots filled to the brim in your mental picture, you'll remember one other thing. Not only did God act, but He acted abundantly. God blesses and moves into action to protect you, to restore your faith, to strengthen you, to uphold you, to nourish you. He doesn't let you just "sneak by" and provide the minimum just to get you through. He blesses you *abundantly*! What a beautiful recollection that snapshot can be! It reminds you to praise God. It reminds you to be patient as you wait upon Him. It reminds you to thank Him for all that He abundantly does for you.

As you think back to this particular wedding, you may want to take some other snapshots as other things occur to you. Maybe you will want to photograph the host, or the wine steward, or the servants, or the bride and groom, and note their reactions of awe, amazement, gratitude, and praise. And these responses will be yours too, as you patiently wait for God's love to act in your life.

Remember: Wait on the Lord.
In His own time and way,
He will act for your good.
He will bless you abundantly!

25

You

Yes, you are really important. Take a look at 1 Peter 2:9.

> But you are the chosen race, the King's priests, the holy nation, God's own people, chosen to proclaim the wonderful acts of God, who called you from the darkness into His own marvelous light (TEV).

Some people who are neglected, overlooked, or discriminated against reach the point where they really wonder whether they are worth anything at all. You know it can get mighty lonely and tiresome living in drudgery each day without really feeling good about yourself.

I think it's time to say a word to those people who do not have very much self-esteem. It's time to say a word to those who are wondering whether life is worth living.

Are you wondering whether anyone cares? If you're feeling low right now, this message is for you. *I want you to know how much God loves you and how important you are to God*! Each individual counts! Each person is so precious and so valuable to God that He sent His own Son, Jesus Christ, to suffer and die on the cross *just for you.*

Now that's the remarkable thing about God's love. He loves you so much that He sent His Son to be your Savior. Once in awhile you get the impression, when people talk about Jesus Christ being the Savior of the world, that He went ahead and did it because there were large numbers involved. Well that misses the point entirely. The point of the Gospel message is that God would have done that even if *you* were the only one. That's how much He loves *you.*

Let your whole self-esteem return. Now I'm not talking about pride. I'm talking about a healthy God-pleasing value that you would put on yourself, self-esteem. Take a look again at those words in 1 Peter 2:9: "You are the chosen race"(TEV).

You know how disappointing it is when you are not chosen. I grew up in Iowa in the little town of Charter Oak. Almost every weekend I went roller skating, as did most of my fellow high school friends. During the evening there would be "skates" that were "ladies' choices" and "men's choices." There were usually more girls than fellows. So when it was a "men's choice," there would always be girls that were not chosen. They would be left just standing there. What a terrible feeling!

Have you ever been with a group trying to get a game of baseball, basketball, or soccer together? The two "captains" begin choosing players. The selection process goes on and neither has yet chosen you. It makes you feel like quitting doesn't it? We all know how it feels to be left out. But here God is saying, "I have chosen you." Boy, that's fantastic! Chosen by God! You! And me!

Then He goes on to say, "You are royal priests." If you have faith in the Lord Jesus Christ and you believe that Jesus is your personal Savior, then God has made you a priest— one of His royal priesthood. Nothing and no one stands between you and God. There are no mediators. Jesus Christ Himself is the mediator and you have direct access to Him. You are His royal priest. He wants you to represent Him to the world. What a calling! What a fantastic privilege to be a priest of God! You are a holy nation. You are holy because you have been forgiven and because your sins have been taken away. God has called you to be His own.

Look at the next phrase, "You are God's own people." Now I really hope that God's Holy Spirit is letting that sink in and penetrate to that brain and down there into your heart so that feeling, that understanding, and that awareness sinks in when you hear *you are God's own person*. God loves you! He sent you a Savior, His Son Jesus Christ, and God is going to take care of you. If you hang on and believe in Him, He is going to give you life eternal.

Now God has called us, each one of us, to be that special kind of person. He wants us to declare His wonderful works to the world. In this way, other people who are feeling just as badly as some of you were when you started reading this message, can have a new lease on life, a new purpose, and a new hope.

I really hope that each of you recognizes how terribly important you are to God; how much love He has for you, and that He has called you to be His own. He has chosen you—you are His royal priest to do His will. You are holy because of His forgiveness. You are His very own person. He created you. He has taken care of you. He sent you a Redeemer in His Son, Jesus Christ. He has delivered you from sin through forgiveness, and He wants to bless you and use you as He guides you day-by-day in your life.

Well, there is no reason then for a person to look down at himself or herself to be discouraged in his or her own personality. There should be a healthy self-respect (not arrogance or pride). Each of us should have a quiet confidence and be comforted knowing *I belong to God. God has chosen me*!

26

Gifts

Let's look at three of God's gifts to us: peace, prosperity, and perpetuity.

Peace. Everybody wants peace! We would like to have peace with God so that we would not have to fear Him. We would like to have peace with our fellowman so that we could live in a relatively calm society, free from war. We would like to have peace in our personal relationships with relatives and friends so that there could be a harmony in our lives. We would like to have peace with ourselves so that we could be free from a troubled conscience and sleepless nights.

How can we find peace? God has provided us the answer! And it is the *only* answer. He has given us His Good News. We refer to the message of the Gospel in 1 Corinthians 15, where we are told about this Good News. In the opening four verses, Paul describes for us the heart of the Gospel. He repeats for us the suffering and death of Christ and His resurrection. Christ Himself is the Good News. His coming to suffer in our place upon the cross washed away all of our sins. His resurrection from the dead established that everything had been completed to make mankind right with God once again.

In that simple, yet all important, message is contained the essence of peace. Christ restored our relationship with the Father. We need no longer fear a righteous God because in His Son He has made us righteous, holy, and free from sin. We have actually been made saints of God through faith in Jesus Christ. God tells us that through the work of His Son, our sins have been removed from His sight as far as the east is from the west, and they will be remembered no more. So we are at peace with God.

The peace that God offers us is a peace that goes beyond ourselves and actually establishes a peaceful relationship with our fellowman. We are given the power, by Christ living in us, to act toward our fellowman in the same way that Christ has shown us love. In other words, we are to pass on the love that Christ has shown us. This will show itself in a forgiving attitude and in looking at other people through the eyes of Christ.

And we will be at peace with ourselves. Since our sins have been forgiven and our guilt washed away, there is no longer a need for a burdened conscience. Since our guilt has been paid by Christ, there is no need for self-inflicted worry or punishment. When a person is truly free, he or she can be at peace—there is nothing to fear.

Prosperity. In Rom. 1:16 Paul says that he is not ashamed of the Gospel of Christ, for it is the power of God to bring us to salvation. God's power is present in the lives of His people. It is the same power that resurrected Christ from the dead. God's Holy Spirit is still at work performing miracles and transforming lives every day.

It is God's intent that His people lead lives that are filled with joy and contentment. We must understand that God's people view prosperity from a different point of view than the world does. The world thinks only of materialism—a self-serving selfish type of gaining advantage and gaining wealth, etc. In Biblical terms, a person could possess the entire world and still not be happy or content. It is quite easy to see this in the lives of wealthy people. So often their wealth has brought them only more despair and loneliness. Perhaps the movie industry idols can serve as an example of that type of futile pursuit after earthly gains.

God offers a different type of prosperity. As we have already seen, He offers us peace. No amount of money can purchase that gift. He also offers us purpose in life. It is a beautiful thing to know why you are here and how God is using you in His eternal plan. Contentment is a blessing that God also offers His people. God desires His people to have fullness of life—a prosperity that the world knows nothing about.

God's power provides these marvelous gifts. He leads the lives of His people day by day. He even works out those evil things that approach us and inflict our lives with pain and suffering and turns them into blessings. Truly God's people are prosperous.

Perpetuity. The word means never ending, always and always, eternal. Even the best of lives would be futile if at their end there was nothing more. That thought was summarized well in a popular song some years ago, "Is That All There Is?" One of the great aspects of God's Good News through His Son Jesus Christ is that He is not only concerned with our lives here and now, but He has also prepared eternal life for us. God wants His people to live forever. That was His original plan also. Then sin came into the lives of disobedient mankind, and with it came things like death and everything else that is evil.

God has assured His followers that He is going to restore a perfect life for us in heaven. It will be completely free from sin. Sin will not be allowed. In that perfection there will once again be no death, aging, despair, fatigue, worry, infirmities, confusion, sorrow, or anything else that has disrupted God's plan for His people. It will be perfect! And our joy will be complete!

If you were able to take your happiest moment here on earth and multiply it a million times, you would still not have the perfection of joy that will be ours every moment of eternity. It is beyond the grasp of man's ability to understand. It is so far above our human concepts and thinking that we can only accept and trust God to fulfill and do for us what He has promised. It will be positively fantastic!

Peace, prosperity, and perpetuity . . . and the greatest of these gifts is perpetuity!

So, in Christ, we have found the total answer. There is no more! Through His suffering and death for us, we are at peace with our Father in heaven.

Through Christ's presence in our lives and the power of His Holy Spirit, we have lives that are filled with meaning, purpose, and joy. It should be obvious that the joy we are speaking of is a joy that can even shine through sorrows and difficulties. It is a joy that can come only from Christ.

In Christ Jesus we have not only found the meaning and purpose and fullness of life here, but we have found life eternal. He is not only our Lord, but also our Savior! Those who believe in Him will live forever!

27

Priorities

What's really important in our lives? And what should really be of first importance to us? Let's look at that beautiful verse from Matt. 6:33: "But seek first His kingdom and His righteousness, and all these other things shall be yours as well."

God is saying that He wants top priority in our lives. He wants first place. He will not share that spot with anything or anyone else. We are to put Him first and worship Him as the only true God. And we are to seek His righteousness. That means we need to be made right with God in order to receive His forgiveness. That's only possible through His Son Jesus Christ. Jesus is the only Savior. Therefore, only through Him, through His suffering and death, and our accepting Him as our personal savior, can we receive forgiveness for all of our sins. That's what makes us right with God. Many times the pursuit of money or some other earthly goal gets in the way of our putting God first in our lives. You know it really is a terrible thing when people get so wrapped up in seeking a name for themselves, a higher income, or some career goal that they have no time to worship and praise the Lord. Whatever it is you work and slave for, whatever it is you refuse to give up—that is really your god. If your priorities are out of whack, you're worshiping idols or false gods. Get your priorities straight! Put the true God in first place in your life.

Maybe you're worshiping money or something else and have a false idol. Well, break those habits! We can break those binds that try to rule and dominate us. Let's take charge of our lives and put in the first priority our Lord Jesus Christ, true God, and the Father and the Holy Spirit. If we seek His righteousness, walk with Him, ask His forgiveness, get into

His Word, make witnesses to those who do not yet know Christ, and serve Him, our lives are going to be the kind that the world will take notice of. People will notice that we show a great deal of love instead of retaliation, a great deal of giving instead of demanding attention from others, a great deal of patience instead of anger and hostility. All of those traits will be a witness to our faith.

Give extremely high priority to such things as teaching your children to love the Lord, worship, serving the Lord, and living your life in a quiet and peaceful way. Set aside time to make a witness, to study God's Word, and to serve the Lord by serving your fellow man.

I hope you will read Matt. 6:33, commit it to memory, and live by it. Put God first in your life. He isn't going to forget you. He will bless you. He will take care of you. Just as He says, "All these other things will be yours as well."

28

Discipleship

Discipleship is vastly more important than church membership. With all the emphasis that is placed on church membership and membership rolls, the impression is left that being on a membership list is equivalent to being a Christian. Nothing could be more false! It is possible to be on a membership roll and not even be a Christian. Christ was constantly warning "members" of the organized religion of His day that it was not enough to pay lip service to Him. He demanded commitment! Not everyone that said, "Lord, Lord," was going to make it—only those who backed up their confession with a sincere heartfelt commitment of their life. Christ didn't want "hearers" only, He wanted "doers." His parable of the ten virgins clearly demonstrated that fact. Each of the young women had lamps, each had oil, each was waiting for the bridegroom—yet half of them didn't make it.

I'm not trying to strike despair or doubt into your hearts. Certainly every believer in Jesus Christ can be completely assured of his or her salvation. Even the weakest Christian can take comfort in that certainty! God in His mercy will save all those who come to Him in faith through Christ.

What I am trying to reveal is how far short we fall compared to what God expects. This realization should lead us to repentance. In repentance we will seek God's strengthening and enabling power to lift us up and make us more like the people He wants us to be. In repentance we will be open to the working of the Holy Spirit. Spiritual growth will be the result.

Let's read what Christ says about discipleship:

> Luke 14:27: And anyone who does not carry his cross and follow me cannot be my disciple (NIV).

The cross referred to here is not illness or handicaps. It is the burden that comes to us in the form of rejection, disapproval, and mockery because of our witness to Christ. We often sense that a bold witness on our part would alienate us from our friends, so we remain silent. As a result, we have no cross to bear. Yet, Christ says that to be His disciples we must take up our cross and be willing to suffer the consequences of a strong Christian witness to the world.

> Luke 14:33: In the same way, any of you who does not give up everything he has cannot be my disciple (NIV).

Isn't that something! We are literally to be ready to give up everything for God. Whatever we refuse to give up is really our god. What we refuse to part with for the sake of God has a higher priority in our life—that is what we really worship. Luther was so correct when he pointed out that we are all guilty of idolatry. We need to repent! Our priorities will be rearranged. Once again, He will be lifted up as our Lord and Savior. Our focus will be realigned, and we will worship and praise Him as true God. Then our actions will be declarations of worship and praise.

> John 8:31: To the Jews who had believed him, Jesus said, "If you hold to my teaching, you are really my disciples" (NIV).

You see, God assumes that we know His will. That is why He requires us to be obedient to it. Where does that leave the "inactive" member? They don't read God's Word, they don't attend Bible study classes, they don't thirst after and long for God's Word. So how can they know what it says?

(At this point someone is bound to say, "But a person can go to church every Sunday, attend Bible class, read God's Word daily, and still go to hell. Just by doing those things you do not become a Christian. What about the hypocrites?")

I agree. Hopefully, we all know and understand the danger. But let's not get sidetracked from the important truth that we are trying to learn. We are discussing the apathetic, uncommitted, inactive, complacent child of God who has been lulled into thinking he or she is a Christian merely by having his or her name on some church membership list.

It's difficult to talk about commitment and growth because weak and insecure Christians will find themselves overwhelmed. But Christ never "watered down" His call to obedience and commitment. Of course, we know we will fail and never reach perfection. He knows that too. That is why He offers us daily forgiveness. But we are to continue to strive, we are to continue to battle against sin, we are to continue to yearn and work toward a more God-pleasing life. That will occur only when we are aware of our sins and have been moved to repentance.

> John 13:35: All men will know that you are my
> disciples, if you love one another (NIV).

How do we stack up here? What about the cursing, swearing, yelling, and fighting that takes place in our homes? What about the alienation of affection, and the silent treatment? The truth is that we not only find these things present in many of the homes of church members, but we also find it quite frequently in the church.

(Voice of the dissident: "Sure we do! Don't you know that we are all sinners?")

Again I agree with the dissenter. As a matter of fact, we make it clear that anyone wanting to join our parish must be a sinner. Anyone claiming perfection would not fit in with the rest of us sinners. But we are not complacent or smug. We want to grow spiritually, and therefore we strive to improve. Love needs to grow! And if it's alive and "of God," it will grow.

What a fantastic warmth, acceptance, and love would be found in the church if those who claim Christ as their Lord would show and practice more love toward one another.

> John 15:8: This is to my Father's glory, that you

bear much fruit, showing yourselves to be my disciples (NIV).

Notice that Christ wants *much* fruit. We have a great God! Frequently our plans and level of expectations for things to be accomplished do not reveal this greatness. We need to dream bigger! We need to think bigger! We need to plan bigger. We need to call on God more! Let's repent and ask our heavenly Father to take us in His hands and reshape us into *disciples*. Let's stop talking about membership lists and let's start making disciples in fulfillment of our Lord's command in Matthew 28!

29

Wait

Wait is a troublesome word. No one likes to wait. As a matter of fact, we've become almost an "instant society." We have instant breakfast, instant replay, and instant cooking with our microwave ovens—simply "zap it," and it's done. We all know how irritable we can become if we feel we are waiting a little too long to be seated in a restaurant. Some of us will actually leave if we feel we have to wait too long. We know how annoyed we get when we have to wait in line, even if it is for something unimportant. We are basically impatient people.

When we talk about waiting, it makes us stop and think. And when the Bible speaks of "waiting on the Lord," then we have to be really thinking because we are dealing in a spiritual dimension. (See Ps. 27:14; Ps. 62:5; Prov. 20:22; and Is. 40:29–31.) Now when we "wait upon the Lord," it means that we have turned something over to God, asking for His blessing and an answer to our needs. If at first it seems that the Lord is hesitant or unwilling to answer, we need to wait upon Him and remind ourselves spiritually that His time is not our time, His ways are not our ways, and He alone knows what and *when* is best. So patiently, in faith, we wait for Him to act in our lives.

There is an account in the Bible that I believe demonstrates this type of waiting that we are speaking of. It's in Luke 8. It begins at verse 8 with the account of a man named Jairus who comes to Jesus with a specific problem. He has a little daughter about 12-years-old who is seriously ill and near death. Jairus, along with the rest of the crowd, had been waiting patiently. Finally, Jesus arrives and, through the discourse, we see that Jairus has been able to persuade Jesus to come with Him and help. Now you can picture the crowd; more than likely it was a large throng of people. Jairus was probably using his elbows trying to lead the way with Jesus following him so that they could get out of the press of the crowd. After all of his waiting, Jairus has finally succeeded and Jesus is now coming with him. But as he looks back over his shoulder, he notices that Jesus is no longer following. He has been sidetracked and has stopped for a discussion with someone else.

Can you imagine the feeling within Jairus? Somebody else has pressed in on Jesus for His time and consideration. Imagine what it would be like if you were speaking to your pastor on Sunday morning about some personal problem and, in the middle of your conversation, some other member interrupts. Before you know what's happening, the pastor is deeply involved with the other person, and you are left standing there, apparently forgotten. That is what happened to Jairus. He must have been overwhelmed with impatience—first the waiting and now someone else is dominating Jesus' time— and all this while he knows that his little daughter is dying. Now put yourself in that situation and ask yourself how calm and patient you would have been.

We read about the strange event that sidetracked Jesus in verses 43–47. If you would have heard that conversation with Jesus and the crowd, you would have thought, "My goodness, what kind of nonsense is this?", because what Jesus said doesn't appear to make any sense at all. Jesus says, "Someone touched Me. Who touched Me?" Now remember, there is a large throng of people—probably each one touching someone else—and all pressing and clamoring to get Jesus' attention. So what an unusual statement, "Who touched me? Someone touched me." We see Jesus turning and then we hear the dialogue between Him and the woman who was healed. In verse 48 He says to her, "Your faith has made you well; go in peace."

And all this while Jairus is waiting. In the meantime, while this is going on, a messenger comes to Jairus and says, "As a matter of fact, it's too late. You might as well not bother now because your daughter has passed away. She is dead."

I believe that at that point most of us, if we'd have been in Jairus' situation, would have given up. We would have said, "There is no way I'm going to wait upon the Lord any longer. He has failed me. He has turned to others instead. He hasn't seen the seriousness of my problem, and He hasn't helped me." We probably would've quit right then and there. But not Jairus. The Lord reassures him, continues with him to his home, and miraculously raises his daughter from the dead. So Jairus' patience and waiting were rewarded.

The application in our lives is very clear. We sometimes feel that our problems are overwhelming—just as Jairus did. Our concern for a fellow member of our family or for ourselves is so shattering that we are convinced that a solution must be found immediately. And then when we experience what appears to us to be a long period of waiting for our Lord to answer our prayers, we become impatient and probably rebellious and resentful. We then question, like King David did at times in his life, whether God really does love us, whether He really is going to interfere in the course of events and help us. So, in our impatience, we become rebellious almost to the point where we begin to lose our faith and trust in God.

In contrast to that attitude, which is very negative and very unloving toward God, we should learn from the patience and waiting of Jairus. We ought to trust God enough to know that He never lets His people down, that He never fails to help, and that He never misses an opportunity. And the timing, which He alone knows, is best. It may not suit our needs, or our feelings, or our way or manner of doing things, but God knows best. Faith and trust in God is holding on at precisely those times when it seems as though everything is lost.

Just as surely as God chose the correct moment in time for His Son to come to earth—to suffer, die, and rise as our Savior—so also He knows the best timing for our lives.

So the Biblical imperative of "waiting upon the Lord" becomes a watchword for our Christian life.

To wait means to trust.

To wait means to believe.

To wait means to have hope.

To wait is a confession of faith that God knows our needs, that He is concerned about them, and that He has the power to solve them—and He will do so in a way that is always to our benefit.

I am sure that you, along with me, need to repent of impatience. At times we have resented waiting upon the Lord because it interfered with our timetable or the things that we felt were important.

If you are in a situation today where you are feeling the need for help, wait patiently and trust in the Lord. And if you don't happen to be in this situation of waiting, tuck this message away in your mind and in your heart. Remember the next time you feel that everything is going wrong, or you feel rejected or deserted or unloved, "wait on the Lord."

One of the great classic accounts in the Bible which deals with a resurrection is this account of Jairus and his daughter in Luke 8. Throughout the gospels we find the miracles of our Lord as a reminder that He has power over all things.

Now He may choose a way in your case and in your life that may seem for a moment to be unproductive. But it could be just like the faceting of a diamond. You may need to be "polished" a little more. You may need to have some aspects of your life disciplined so that you grow closer to the Lord. Or it may be that repentance is necessary in your life. He will do whatever is best for you.

His holy name be praised as we wait upon Him to act in our lives!

30

Questions

Most of us have questions that come into our minds—questions about our life, about why certain things happen. In fact, we frequently find ourselves even questioning God.

Well, let's take a look at this subject. Please read John 6:1–14. The verse I'd like to focus on is verse 6 (tucked right in the middle of the whole account of the feeding of the 5,000) where we are told that Jesus asked Philip a question. "This He said to test him, for He Himself knew what He would do."

Let's have that verse sink in a little bit and make sure that we understand it. We know that there was a great multitude of people gathered around and Jesus had been teaching. Then it came time to eat, and all of a sudden the apparent problem was recognized—there was no food around the area.

They were close to Bethsaida, a little community right along the shoreline of the Sea of Galilee. I can just picture in my mind the many times I've seen that beautiful Sea of Galilee and the area where this miracle took place. It is incredibly beautiful—but it's hard to describe. The little Sea of Galilee is about nine miles long, three or four miles across, and surrounded by mountains. The northern shoreline is a beautiful plush area where there has been a lot of irrigation so there are fruit trees and much greenery. A beautiful little church on the hillside commemorates this miracle.

By the way, this is where Philip came from. This was Philip's region, and he may have known some of the people in this crowd. So he had a special concern—how are we going to feed these people? How are we going to solve this problem? Well, Jesus put a question to him. Let me paraphrase it. "What do you think we should do, Philip? How can we solve this problem?" And then we are told that Jesus asked that question found in verse 6. He didn't ask it because He needed to find out where to get the food. The purpose of the question was to increase the faith of Philip, to give Philip an opportunity to grow in faith.

But, of course, Philip didn't realize that. If he would have thought for just a moment, he would have said, "Well, Lord, I really don't know, but certainly You do!" As a matter of fact, some commentators have tried to pick up on the thought that maybe Philip was very low on faith, and that maybe of all the disciples, he needed to be brought along a little bit and taught the necessity of depending upon the Lord more than he was doing. Well, we can't say that for sure, but obviously his faith did need strengthening.

So he didn't respond in the right way, as would certainly be the case with most of us as well. He began by analyzing the situation and sized up the circumstances on a human level. "How are we going to be able to meet the need? Well, my conclusion is we simply do not have enough money to buy the food that we need. There just isn't any way to make ends meet, and it can't be done." It's so typically human, isn't it? There is the Lord God Almighty right in front of him, and he's looking for a human solution rather than responding in faith and saying, "Lord, you can solve it. You can do all things. We have seen You perform miracles and acknowledge You to be the Son of God."

Andrew comes into the picture too. In verse 8 he goes at it a little differently. He sizes up the situation and says, "Well, we do have five loaves of bread and two fish here." You can see he's very pragmatic and getting right to the point. He's saying, "I've taken a little survey of the situation and this is what I see." Philip was looking at the whole overwhelming task to be done and concluded it couldn't be done. Andrew was saying, "Well, let's make a start and see what we have." His was a slightly different approach administratively, and yet his conclusion was the same—it can't be done.

So often when questions come up in our lives, instead of realizing that the burden, need, crisis, or moment of despair is really God's way of calling us to faith, we begin to hunt for earthly solutions. Maybe you go at it the way Philip did, or maybe you go at it the way Andrew did, or maybe you have your own way of trying to find an earthly solution. You'll try all of your resources before your eyes are opened to respond, "Lord, Lord, You can do it. Of course You can! You can solve any problem in my life, if You so choose."

Getting back to the problem of feeding the 5,000, we see how God abundantly blessed. God knew in His Son, Jesus Christ, just exactly what He was going to do, just when and just how the entire need could be completely met. As a matter of fact, the need was met in such an abundant way that there were even going to be leftovers.

I would like to have you join me in double-checking the questions that are on your mind: Questions about your job, family, marriage, children, illness, pain, or about any kind of situation you're in—a crisis, a need, a sorrow, a burden, anything. For a moment, stop dealing with it on a human level. I don't mean to give up. I don't mean that at all. God certainly expects us to apply ourselves and our energies and talents and determination. We all understand and know that God doesn't expect us to pray for food to come down from heaven and just land on our empty table. He expects us to use the energy and blessings and talents He has given us to go out and work in answering those prayers.

He also wants us to step back for a moment and consider whether all we are doing is looking at the human resources, but missing the very point that Jesus had in mind. And we don't have to guess at this. We don't have to say, "I wonder why Jesus asked Philip the question." We're told why in verse 6. We're told it was for Philip's benefit. It wasn't that Jesus needed an answer. Philip needed help—not Jesus. And the need wasn't to find food; the need was to create a deeper faith in Philip.

And so I ask you—with all the questions running through your mind and heart, as they certainly do in my life also—to just pause and say, "Wait a minute, wait a minute!" Who leads and guides and directs my life? Who is my Lord and Savior? Who do I trust to be the true Son of God? Whom do I acknowledge to be the One who died on the cross for my sins? Who is this?! He is none other than God Himself, and as such, He is able to answer all my needs and solve all of my problems. And not only is He *able*, but He *will* because He loves me!

How will He do it? Maybe He will choose that I suffer longer. Maybe He will choose that the answer will come later. Maybe He will choose that the answer is going to be something that I feel is wrong. And yet He assures me He will always answer all of my questions in the very best way, the most beneficial for me, and always as a blessing because He is a loving God, and He loves those who trust in Him.

So consider Philip and Andrew and the question they were struggling with in light of the answer that God had already prepared, and you will also discover that God has an answer for you. He knows *what* He is going to do, He knows *when* He is going to do it, He knows *how* He's going to do it, and I can assure you, friend, He is going to do it abundantly. He will be with you!

31

Hope

St. Paul was aware of the fact that it is our natural inclination to get fed up, tired, disgusted, and feel like quitting. If anyone could have had those feelings or those moods, it would have been St. Paul. Look at how utterly discouraging things were for him from time to time. Yet here is what he wrote to the Galatians:

> So let us not become tired of doing good; for if we do not give up, the time will come when we will reap the harvest (Gal. 6:9 TEV).

There is hope. One author has paraphrased this text by saying the Greek words would be better translated, "Don't give up in beautiful doing." Do what is beautiful.

Now let's be realistic. There are going to be times when you're going to say, "I wonder if it's worth it?" You've been trying to witness to a relative, or you've been trying to talk to your teenager, or you've been trying to make some headway with that neighbor in terms of his or her life, and yet it looks as if you're up against a stone wall. And you say to yourself, "I don't know. I'm just not getting anywhere." You're disgusted. You feel like quitting. Well, at those times, reread Gal. 6:9 and let that text keep you going.

God gives us a basis for understanding what His command and request are all about. He doesn't just say something and then leave us to wonder why He is saying, "Hang in there." He says that in due time, at the right time, at precisely the time that He decides is the very best for us, "there will come a harvest." It will be a blessed harvest. It will be a harvest of spiritual good. Good things will come. Here is how the harvest is described in Gal. 6:7–8:

> Do not deceive yourselves; no one makes a fool of God. A person will reap exactly what he plants. If he plants in the field of his natural desires, from it he will gather the harvest of death; if he plants in the field of the Spirit, from the Spirit he will gather the harvest of eternal life (TEV).

You know that one of the laws of nature that God has given us is that you always reap what you sow. When you plant flower seeds, you're not going to get corn, you're going to get flowers. Whatever you plant—carrots, potatoes, etc.—that's what you will get.

The reminder here is that if you sow evil—destruction, jealousy, envy, pride—the harvest is going to come back with all of that maliciousness piled and heaped upon you. The harvest will be God's judgment.

But if you sow the fruit of the Spirit (read Gal. 5:22)—love, joy, peace, patience, kindness, goodness, faithfulness, gentleness, and self-control—the harvest will be a blessed one. That is God's promise. That is a great message.

What a comfort that message gives to those who are leading a pious and holy life; those who have been praying so long and so hard and wondering whether or not things will ever change; wondering whether God knows their needs and will take action. The answer is yes, yes, yes! God knows my needs. God knows your needs. He is observing. He is watching. He cares and He will give a harvest. He will grant a blessing if you don't give up.

There are always a lot of starters for every race. Some of the most popular marathons in recent years have had thousands at the starting line. But as the race progresses, one by one many hundreds drop out. They fall by the wayside.

I remember working in the harvest fields in Rochelle, Illinois, when I was in college. During the summer season we'd go out and manually pitchfork pea vines onto wagons. I remember very well that a truck would arrive daily at about

11:30 a.m. with new recruits to replace those who had caved in or given up. Every day three of four would quit and get on that truck.

Those first days were the roughest ones because we were so out of shape. We literally got blisters inside of blisters. It was probably the hardest any of us had ever worked in our lives. I remember watching that truck drive up every day and recall the struggle I went through. I kept telling myself, "There is no way on the face of this earth that I'm going to give up. I'm not quitting!"

That's the kind of attitude we should have spiritually. We have the most tremendous resource of God's Holy Spirit at our disposal. We have His sacred meal in the Lord's Supper for our strengthening and support. We have God's Word for our daily enrichment and encouragement. And we have the continuing presence of Jesus Christ in our lives!

St. Paul is advising us correctly. There is hope. Don't give up. Don't quit. Hang in there.

And be patient. A farmer doesn't plant corn and then wonder the next morning why it isn't sticking out of the ground already. It takes time.

So, dear friends, keep doing what is good. Keep doing what is beautiful. Keep doing what is pleasing to God. You may not have seen the harvest yet, but it's coming. That is God's promise!

PART 3

Coping: Our Relationship with Others

(Relational)

32

Show and Tell

We are invited by God to tell the world about His goodness and His love, and especially that it has a Savior in God's own Son, Jesus Christ.

Now those in whom God has worked faith and whom He has called as His own children and made heirs of eternal life are the people He expects to do the telling.

I can remember in school when we had "Show and Tell." Each child was to make his or her own little presentation to the class. The children could bring a pet or something from home that they treasured and really loved. They would then show it to the class and tell something about it. Many years later I would see my own children leaving for school carrying an item they were going to use for their own "Show and Tell" period.

God says to us, "I want you to 'show and tell.' I want you to show the world that there is something different about you now that I have entered your life and made you My children." The real problem with the Christian church is that too often its members are not very different from the world around them. If we don't show the world the difference, why should the world be inclined to want to hear what we have to say. It was easy to know who the Christians were during the persecutions that occurred in the early New Testament church era. There weren't as many Christians, perhaps, but those who remained faithful were much stronger. You could see it in their lives. You could notice the enormous difference between them and the people of the world around them.

Now that contrast has become quite blurred. It's probably too easy today to become a member of a church. In some churches you can simply walk in and say, "Hey, I want to be a member." Some don't require courses of instruction or even inquire about a person's beliefs. As a result, one can be very worldly and not believe too many basic things at all, and still be a member of a Christian church. Many of these "members" are not really followers of Christ. They go out into the world and appear exactly like unbelievers. The world hears them cursing and swearing just like they do. The world sees them living in all kinds of sin just like they do, and there is no distinctive difference between "Christians" and the world. No wonder the witness of the church has become blurred and fuzzy to the point where we don't really make that great an impact on the world around us.

But God would like it to be different. He would like each one of the people He has called to Himself by the power of His Holy Spirit to become a walking testimony, a living example of what it means to be Christlike, a follower of Christ.

We should be showing the world that we are *different*. We ought to have a greater degree of love. We ought to have a greater degree of patience. We ought to have *different* priorities and goals, reflecting love. We ought to have a *different* attitude toward the world than worldly people do. We ought to have a *different* attitude toward material possessions, knowing that these are not our goal in life because we are merely passing through on our way to our heavenly home. We ought to have a *different* kind of family life than the worldly people around us. We ought to spend more time training and working with our children. We ought to be quicker to assist someone in trouble. We are to reflect those Christ-like qualities that God has given us in showing us His love through His Son, Jesus Christ.

And along with this *showing*, we also ought to be *telling*. You can imagine how embarrassing it would be if the child held up an object for "Show and Tell," but wouldn't say a word about it. Something would be missing. The object would be on display, and everyone could see it, but there wouldn't be any information to go with it.

So God wants us to *show* by the example of our lives that Christ is present within us. But He wants more than showing.

He also wants us to *tell*. It's not enough to just show your love. You also have to explain, or tell about your love for Jesus so they know *why* you are showing love to them.

I believe one of the most beautiful sections of Scripture that helps us point this out is the penitential Psalm of David, Psalm 51. In this psalm David repents; he asks God to forgive his sins. I believe that if we want to lead a happy life, a life that is filled with peace, we need to repent—to come to Christ and be washed in His blood. I believe that many Christians are not filled with joy and happiness because they carry too many burdens and sins and guilt with them. Even though they know Christ is their Savior, even though they believe they have forgiveness, they do not rejoice. I believe it's important to repent daily, and even frequently throughout the day, to be constantly living in the peace which God gives, and be filled with the certainty and assurance that our sins have been washed clean by Christ.

In Psalm 51 we see David coming in repentance to God and asking for that cleansing. But he also talks about this *telling* in verses 12–15:

> Restore to me the joy of Thy salvation, and up-
> hold me with a willing spirit. Then I will teach
> transgressors Thy ways, and sinners will return
> to Thee. Deliver me from bloodguiltiness, O God,
> the God of my salvation, and my tongue will sing
> aloud of Thy deliverance. O Lord, open Thou my
> lips, and my mouth shall show forth Thy praise.

Telling is very simple. Anyone can do it. You don't have to memorize a formula. You don't have to memorize sections of the Bible. You don't have to have religious training in order to be able to talk with someone about Christ. And don't let Satan try to intimidate you with, "You don't know what to say and you don't know how to say it." Or "What if you say it the wrong way?" The devil would love to get you thinking that way because then you would never say anything. You would be crippled by fear. You would never open your mouth.

But God wants you to think just the opposite. God says, "You know what I've done for you. You know how I helped you raise your children. You know how I cared for you and provided for you. That's what I want you to praise Me for. Tell others what I have done for you. And above all, if you really know My Son, Jesus Christ, if you know Him personally—that I have forgiven you for His sake—you can certainly tell people about that. Tell the world you have a God who loves you."

Tell the world what God has done for you. Tell the world that He sent His Son to the cross for you, that He suffered and died for you. You can tell them that. And you can hold out Jesus to them because Jesus wants them to believe in Him too, and He offers them that same forgiveness and that same love.

So we are to *show* the world our love in Jesus Christ, but we are also to *tell* the world about God's offer of forgiveness. We are really to *show and tell*.

Quickly

God has told us that we are to go quickly about the task of bringing His Word to the world. We should have a sense of urgency because Judgment Day could come anytime—it could come today!

Nowadays it seems almost everyone is talking about the end of the world. When I was in a bookstore recently, I saw a new edition of the works of Nostradamus, the 16th-century astrologer. The title of the paperback was "Nostradamus Predicts the End of the World Before the Year 2000." There are people who believe in such predictions.

Then there are scientists and demographers who say the world's population is growing at an alarming rate, and we'll get to the point where we'll have more people than our planet can support.

There are many others who have been predicting for years that the end of the world will come through nuclear holocaust.

It's interesting to me that many radio and TV preachers believe that the end of the world will come in their lifetimes.

How the world will end and when it will end is not really a problem for the Christian church. After all, we Christians believe the Lord Jesus Christ is our Savior. He has forgiven our sins. We are saved regardless of whether the Lord is coming today, tomorrow, 30 or 300 years from now.

Some denominations believe the references in Revelation, Daniel, and Ezekiel are to be taken literally. They interpret each verse in a way that refers to today's events and predict the future accordingly. Other denominations regard those same verses and prophecies as having been fulfilled long ago, or as references to those things which will take place on Judgment Day itself. They believe the language and numbers used are symbolic and not intended to be taken literally.

I don't think it makes a whole lot of difference as far as a person's salvation is concerned, as to what he or she believes regarding when the end of the world will come. What troubles me is how this must sound to the unbeliever. If unbelievers hear Christians saying that you'll know when Judgment Day is imminent because there will be signs—first a war in Israel, then this and that will happen—they are left with the impression that they still have lots of time to repent.

The Bible teaches that Judgment Day will come when it's least expected—not when everyone is looking for it and saying, "It's probably going to be this week." That is when it is *least* likely to come. It will come like a thief in the night (1 Thess. 5:2) when no one is expecting it.

We also know from reading the Scriptures that Judgment Day could come *today*, right now, this minute, and therefore, the message to the unbeliever ought to be that *now* is the time to repent (2 Cor. 6:2), as the Bible clearly teaches. The unbeliever may not have another five or 10 or 20 years. Today is the day to become God's child and to receive the gift of eternal life.

But this decision shouldn't be made out of fear or because of threats. It ought to be a decision that is recognized as God's work of faith in the heart. It is God who rescues you. It is God who sends His Holy Spirit into your heart and transforms you into a new creature (2 Cor. 5:17). That new creature is brought about because He has washed away your sins and forgiven every single wrong through the blood of His Son, Jesus Christ.

Some people say, "Hasn't it been a long time since Christ said that He was going to return?" Well, as a matter of fact, no, it hasn't been a long time. You see, time is strictly an earthly thing because of our human limitations. But there is no time with God. God is simply being patient for our sake so that we will bring quickly His message to the world. And look at what He has given us to get that message to the world: modern printing presses, radio, TV, and satellites. God has given us the ability and the means to bring His Word to people all around the world. He has told us to *quickly* get out the message of His eternal, saving love.

So often we run into Christians who seem so lackadaisical. They don't seem to have any fire or zeal or determination to get God's Word out to the world. They don't talk about foreign missions or their neighbor's spiritual needs. I believe this attitude is wrong! God wants to build a fire in the heart of every one of His believers. And He wants to dominate their thinking and time with a fervent desire to bring His Word to the world. That's the only way the world will know about Christ. It's the only way it will find out about Jesus as its Savior. Wherever that Word is preached, proclaimed, and taught, God's Holy Spirit is at work, converting and bringing people to Him, and then transforming their lives. That's the whole purpose and intent of the Christian church.

So I believe God has called you and me to this task. He's made individual assignments. He didn't make us to be His children just for the fun of it. We are to be His people. We are to love Him. We are to respond. We are to respond *quickly* and go about His work with earnestness, zeal, and a sense of commitment. Above all, God has empowered us. He sends His Holy Spirit right along with His Word.

You may think sometimes you are being rejected and not listened to, but that's okay. God wants His Word proclaimed, and as a result, it will bear fruit. Some will reject it, that's true. But others will accept it and find in Jesus Christ their eternal salvation.

That's why we should *quickly* bring God's Word to the world. God loves people and wants them all to be saved (1 Tim. 2:4). He has given us a Savior in His Son, Jesus Christ. Come to Him! Believe in Him and you will be saved! Let's get the message out *quickly*!

34

Someone

I think we need to become a much more personal society. We have heard now for decades about how impersonal our society is. *Someone* can be in need or crying for help, and people ignore it because they are afraid or unwilling to commit themselves. It's time for change, don't you think? The Christian church ought to be the leader. The Bible talks about us being available to someone else, about being "brothers and sisters" to one another. The Scriptures talk about families, the togetherness that we are to have, and the love that we are to show to one another.

In Gal. 6:2 we are told that we are to "bear one another's burdens." So, first of all, let's think about *someone* in particular. There is, no doubt, someone you know who is burdened or has a problem. Maybe there is illness in the family. It might be a shaky situation regarding a job. Maybe you know someone whose children are rebellious, causing them all kinds of problems, or drifting away and not communicating. Or maybe you know someone with a spiritual burden. Maybe they are having doubts and are to the point where they are questioning whether their faith is really true and real. Whatever the burden, God expects us to share it.

Frequently the Christian church is so large and impersonal itself that we don't really get to the point of praying for one another or even discussing with one another how things are going. That is why it's so very important to have small circle groups, so that in these little groups people can actually get to know one another, pray for one another, and share one another's burdens.

In Eph. 4:32 we are told to "be kind to one another." Now

isn't that interesting? I suppose that under God's direction, the authors of the Scriptures knew very well what is in our hearts—how we want to retaliate and repay evil for evil, and how we want to get back at someone who's wronged us. And so we are admonished here, "Hey, that's not the way it's suppose to work. You are to be kind to each other."

And we are to be "tenderhearted." We should put the best construction on what we hear or feel and be willing to overlook someone else's tensions or anger at us. I helped our son with a situation involving an employer years ago. He felt this man kind of "took it out on him" in a way that was unnecessary. I suggested he consider the possibility that there were other tensions in the man's life. Maybe something was causing him to be upset or at that moment to be a little bit unreasonable. And, if at such a moment, we can be considerate and say, "Hey, it's okay. Don't worry about it. I understand," then we are being tenderhearted.

Ephesians 4:32 also mentions "forgiving one another." You know when there is a conflict or problem, if the two people can get together and speak God's love and forgiveness to each other, frequently the problem is resolved. It's only when one of the individuals, or sometimes both, refuse to forgive, refuse to have a loving attitude, refuse to forget, and continue to harbor resentment that the problem will continue to grow and fester and be unresolved. If there is a spirit of love and a willingness to forgive, peace is restored. That's God's promise and it always works. Both people forgive because "God in Christ forgave them."

We are also to submit ourselves to one another. In Eph. 5:21 it says "be subject," and the meaning is to yield or surrender. We are to cooperate with one another and work together to the glory of God. It also speaks of this in terms of married life where two people living closely together need to learn the importance of submitting one to another. There is further reference to husbands and wives in 1 Peter 3:1–9.

We also are to teach and admonish one another. We certainly understand the appropriateness of that when we talk about how we are to raise our children. As they grow and mature, we are to make them aware of what it means to walk with the Lord. And we are not only to do this with our children, but also to one another within the family of God—the Christian church. If we see something going wrong in someone's life and we feel God is moving us to say something, we ought to, in love, admonish and be helpful.

In Heb. 10:24–25, we are told "to stir up one another to love and good works ... encouraging one another." That's very important. Once in awhile when someone is doing something to the glory of God, instead of getting behind it and pushing, we see individuals who seem to resent or be covetous of whatever is being accomplished. Now that is not really a Christian spirit or attitude. Instead, when someone comes up with an idea that God seems to be blessing, let's get behind it and let's push and work together so that great things are done to the glory of God.

I feel that's something the Christian church really needs to work on. So often within congregations there are groups of people who decide what ideas they are going to push and what ideas they like. Maybe it's a building program or the choir or some other organization. Then you have little pockets of people pushing and supporting that, and not supporting other projects. I suppose that's human nature. But Scripture wants us to rise above human nature and to have a spiritual nature that says, "If this project or idea or event is to the glory of God, let's all get behind it and support it and push for it." Wouldn't there be a dramatic change within the kingdom of God if we did that together?

One last exhortation: In 1 Peter 4:10 we are told to minister to one another. "As each has received a gift, employ it for one another, as good stewards of God's varied grace." Someone needs your help. Someone needs your words of encouragement. Someone needs your witness to point them back to Christ and to lead them to repentance. Someone needs you so that they can share a tear because of their loneliness or sorrow. Someone needs to laugh with you and rejoice over a blessing that God has given. *Someone* needs *you*. God has not put you here on this earth in a vacuum, in some sort of a test tube all by yourself, where you're unreachable to the rest of the world. He has put you into a corner of His big wide world with people around you to whom you can give comfort.

God has called you and me to minister to one another, to share one another's burdens, to be tenderhearted, forgiving, kind, submissive, and admonishing and encouraging. I am certain that those who will listen and make themselves available to others for these purposes will be blessed by God. May He give you the mind of Christ and the enlightenment of the Holy Spirit to do His will!

35

Forget

It might seem unusual to talk about *forgetting*. Yet, the Bible stresses both the need to *remember* and the need to *forget*. We are to remember what God has done for us in the past. We are to remember to call upon the name of the Lord. We are to remember to do good works that will glorify His name. We are to remember to be on our guard against Satan. Hopefully, the need for remembering is pretty clear to you and you understand its purpose.

But the need for forgetting may not be so clear to you. Let's look at some of the Bible verses on the subject of forgetting. First, in Phil. 3:7–14 Paul writes,

> But whatever gain I had, I counted as loss for the sake of Christ. Indeed I count everything as loss because of the surpassing worth of knowing Christ Jesus my Lord. For His sake I have suffered the loss of all things, and count them as refuse, in order that I may gain Christ and be found in Him, not having a righteousness of my own, based on law, but that which is through faith in Christ, the righteousness from God that depends on faith; that I may know Him and the power of His resurrection, and may share His sufferings, becoming like Him in His death, that if possible, I may attain the resurrection from the dead. Not that I have already obtained this or am already perfect; but I press on to make it my own, because Christ Jesus has made me His own. Brethren, I do not consider that I have made it my

own; but one thing I do, forgetting what lies behind and straining forward to what lies ahead, I press on toward the goal for the prize of the upward call of God in Christ Jesus.

Isn't that beautiful! The first thing Paul tells us is that we should *forget* all that the world has to offer, because in His opinion, it is nothing—nothing at all. He says he counts it as refuse, as dung, as waste. Because in comparison to having Jesus Christ, all these other things pale into nothingness. If any of these worldly things (possessions, wealth, prestige, fame, power) are standing in the way of a life with Christ, then they must be discarded as if they were garbage. Paul, in another one of his epistles, says, "I don't really even care what other people think of me, as long as I am right with God." These statements remind us to forget worldly pursuits of wealth and prominence. What good are they, or what do they matter before God?

Paul knew he dare not stand before God in his own righteousness and say, "Look, God, this is what I did. Look at all I gained and look at all that I worked on, and look at how important I am." Paul knew better! He knew that coming to God in his own righteousness with his own good works would mean nothing. He could not gain access to heaven by "working" his way because he was not perfect. Paul writes in Phil. 3:9 that he comes in righteousness *which is through faith in Jesus Christ, the righteousness from God that depends on faith.* So we can *forget* our pride, and self-achievements, and wealth. These mean nothing when we are discussing our relationship to God, our forgiveness, or our eternity. To know Jesus Christ and to have His forgiveness of our sins is our righteousness. So, one thing you can *forget* is your worldly pursuits and gains.

The Bible also tells us something else to *forget*. In Matt. 5:38–40, we read that Jesus said, "You have heard that it was said, 'An eye for an eye and a tooth for a tooth,' But I say to you, Do not resist one who is evil. But if any one strikes you on the right cheek, turn to him the other also." And verses 43—45: "You have heard that it was said, 'You shall love your neighbor and hate your enemy.' But I say to you, Love your enemies and pray for those who persecute you."

We should *forget* the hurts and slights and slurs and sins we've experienced at the hands of others. We are to put those thoughts out of our mind. We are not to retaliate or harbor grudges or be resentful. If we do, these very things will harm us. We are to have loving and forgiving hearts—even toward our enemies. Remember God offers forgiveness to them as well as to us. Can we, His children, do less?

So, if you're letting an old wound or hurt dominate your thinking and possess you to the point where you are finding it hard to forgive, or worse yet, you want to "get even," erase it from your memory. Put it out of your mind and heart. Show love and openness to the other person in a way that will show God's love flowing through you.

Here is another aspect the Bible talks about in regard to *forgetting*—God forgets too. Look at Ps. 103:8–12:

> The Lord is merciful and gracious, slow to anger and abounding in steadfast love. He will not always chide, nor will He keep His anger forever. He does not deal with us according to our sins, nor requite us according to our iniquities. For as the heavens are high above the earth, so great is His steadfast love toward those who fear Him; as far as the east is from the west, so far does He remove our transgressions from us.

Here we are told that God puts our forgiven sins as far from Him as the east is from the west.

But what about unrepented sin? Well, God has a way of grinding us down just as He did David, who writes in Psalm 51: "Have mercy ... wash me ... cleanse me ... against Thee, Thee only, have I sinned ... purge me ... hide Thy face from my sins ... deliver me. ... " God leans heavily on us so that we do *not* forget those sins we have *not* repented of. For these we need to come to Him and ask His forgiveness for Jesus' sake.

Even after we have been forgiven, Satan has a nasty trick

of trying to recall our sins to us—even making us doubt God's full and free pardon. Well, the Bible says that once we have been forgiven, those sins can be forgotten. They are to be put behind us.

You notice Paul says that he puts what is past behind him. He doesn't live in the past, saddened by a ruined life or a destroyed future. He says, "I press on toward the goal for the prize of the upward call of God in Jesus Christ." So don't let Satan bother you with past sins! If you have repented of them, God has washed them away. Put them out of your mind and out of your life. Be comforted in knowing that God has made you a new person. He has cleansed you in the blood of His Son, Jesus Christ. What a beautiful, joyful thing it is to know that we can forget the negative, evil things in our past because we have been washed clean.

So *forget* about all those earthly, worldly things. *Forget* about all those injuries and hurts that others may have caused you. *Forget* about those sins that have been forgiven. You have been cleansed by Jesus Christ, and once He forgives, He forgives completely and forgets as well. Strive for "the prize" which is eternity with God! You can rejoice in a new day and a new life!

36

Mending

Let's discuss mending in the sense of sewing something back together or repairing it. In Ephesians 4 you will find a reference to what God expects His church to be. If you read the entire epistle to the Ephesians, you will find various descriptions of the body of Christ, the family of God, the holy Christian church.

The part that I want to focus on in Ephesians 4 begins with verse 11. It is a review of the gifts which God has given to various people. The epistle talks about some of the leaders of the church. There were apostles, prophets, evangelists, pastors, teachers, etc. In verse 12, it says, "they are all for the equipping of the saints." Let's concentrate on that phrase and give some thought to the "equipping of the saints." The Greek word for *equipping* refers to the mending of a net. This is the same Greek word used when the disciples were fishermen and were preparing their nets along the shore of Galilee. They were getting ready for the next day's fishing. They were mending their nets. Holes had to be patched and repaired.

The big question I have for you is: Are you whole? Are you repaired and put back together? Are you functioning properly, or are you a "hole" in the church? Now if you are a hole, a gaping empty spot within that net, you can obviously see that you are part of a problem. As the net is cast into the water, and the catch of fish taken, a hole will permit some fish to escape. The goal will not be achieved because of that hole.

God wants to patch you up, mend you, tie you back together again and make you functional and usable again in His kingdom. He is the great physician! He is the great mender!

He came precisely for that reason—to heal those who need healing, to restore those who need restoring, to strengthen those who are weak. This beautiful Jesus Christ, God's own Son, came precisely for that purpose! As we, the church, function together, we are as sections of a net tied to one another. We are tied in love to one another. We function properly and smoothly together so that God's name will be glorified.

A fishing net has to be prepared and folded a certain way so that the next day it can be cast into the water without becoming tangled. So, also it says in Ephesians 4, that the body of Christ should function in the same way that every part of our own bodies functions as a complete unit. Each part is for the welfare of the body itself. So we the individual members are to be healed and mended and stitched back together again in love so that the "net" of the Gospel can go out into the world. We are to bring people into the church. We are to bring them to the knowledge that Jesus Christ is their Savior. Jesus told His disciples that He no longer would have them be fishermen of fish. He wanted to make them "fishers of men." The mending and healing is the "equipping" of the saints.

God wants us to use every talent and ability we have to glorify His holy name. We are expected to find out what our spiritual gifts are that God has given us. Then we can develop them and use them to God's glory. As we mature in them, and join other Christians, together we can do the will of God. He told us what to do! He has told us what His will is! Jesus gave the Great Commission before He entered heaven. He made it very clear. He didn't say that He was going to give us a number of commissions and then have us pick three or four of them. There is no option! There is only one! He specifically said that the major task of the church—the task which every other function the church is to support and prepare for us—is to reach *all people with God's Word.*

As we go out and make disciples of all people and proclaim His Word, people are going to be saved! That is the goal of God. He wants all men to be saved! Now we know that some are going to reject and deny, but it's God's will that we keep proclaiming it. Keep inviting and keep announcing the love of God for all people. And so, we are in a process of "equipping"—discovering talents and abilities and using them to serve and glorify God.

That is the work of the church. As the church meets together to study God's Word, we grow in our service and praise to God. In Ephesians 5 it says we are to be imitators of God. We are His beloved children. We are to walk in love just as God first loved us. That is to be our sacrifice to God. That is what He expects us to do. There should be no immorality or impurity or covetousness or jealousy or any other thing that disrupts and disturbs the fellowship.

So the Christian church should be in training; it should be disciplined; it should be educated; it should be committed; it should be in prayer; it should be obedient to God. We have one single task to accomplish—bringing God's Word to the world! God's Holy Spirit, through the power of that Word, will bring people to repentance and will cause people to come to know and to believe in Jesus Christ as their personal Lord and Savior!

If you have been a hole in the net of the church and in the proclamation of the Gospel, I hope today you will be mended and repaired. Repent! God in His love will forgive you. He wants you to be in a relationship with your other brothers and sisters in Christ. He wants to use you in His church.

Do yourself a great favor and read the entire Epistle to the Ephesians. It is a very short letter and won't take you long to read. It consists of six short chapters. You will get an insight into what God expects the Christian church to be. If you see yourself as a part of that church, if God has given you the faith, you will then see how God expects you to act in bringing His Word to the world. God will bless your efforts to bring others to Christ!

Fishing

I'm sure some of you have had the experience of waking up on a beautiful summer day—the sun is coming up so beautifully, and the day is going to be just perfect—and you say to yourself, "I feel like going fishing today." In fact, even if you're not a fisherman, you can understand the anticipated pleasure of those who say, "I feel like fishing today."

Well, there is such an incident recorded in John 21, beginning with the first verse. It must have been one of those beautiful days. Peter, who was spokesman for the disciples most of the time, said, "I'm going fishing." No sooner had he said that than the other disciples (Thomas, Nathanael, James, John, and two unnamed) responded, "We'll go with you."

Now, you'll recall that these disciples of our Lord were not going on a recreational fishing jaunt. They were actually professional fishermen. So they knew something about when, where, and how to fish. They knew that the best times to fish would be in the early morning hours, or (in this case) twilight. They remained on the boat in the Sea of Galilee all night.

I can think back to my childhood days when we'd go fishing. I suppose everyone knows that they don't want to be out on the water at noon when the sun is glaring down and the fish aren't likely to bite anyway. And the disciples knew this. They worked all night, but they didn't catch any fish. Now, as the morning light was dawning, the disciples were just about to give up and were probably saying to themselves, "Well, maybe we ought to call it a day." Just then from shore they heard a voice asking, "Young men, have you any fish?" Their response to Jesus (they didn't recognize Him) was, "No, we didn't catch a thing."

Then He said, "Well, cast your net to the right side of the boat and you'll find some." They did as He instructed and, sure enough, they made such a great catch that they were not able to pull in the net!

It's interesting to read this text in the light of our knowledge that Jesus is directing them in their job. He is helping them. You know there are a lot of people who wait for miracles and signs from God. The whole time they are just kind of quietly sitting around waiting. Well, this text speaks of the disciples being out there working. They weren't getting anywhere, but they were trying.

I believe that a good bit of advice to give to anyone who is out there waiting for the blessing of the Lord, or some divine intervention or help, is the fact that God wants us to apply effort and diligence in pursuit of our livelihood. He wants us to make the effort and try. In this Bible text we see God blessing and helping. That same God is in charge today and wants to bless and help all of those who are His people. We shouldn't just sit around an empty table and pray for food to appear. We must be willing to go out and apply the energy and the effort. God will bless. He will provide and give to us what is needed to sustain our lives.

Another interesting thing about this text that we can apply to ourselves is to remember that these disciples who by trade were fishermen, would be sent out by Jesus to become "fishers of men."

When a sower goes out to sow seed, he obviously needs seed. He also needs to know where the field is, and he needs the strength to throw the seed. It was the same with these fishermen. They had to have equipment to work with. They had to have a net and a boat. They had to know something about fishing techniques that worked.

I get the distinct feeling that there are a lot of Christians who are very hesitant to take the initiative when it comes to fishing for people, even though the Lord is standing on the shoreline offering the advice and the help. He is telling us which way to go. He might be telling us to speak to an uncle or aunt or a brother or sister. We feel the tug and the pull at our heart that God wants us to say something, but we refuse to cast the net. We refuse because we are afraid of what they might say or how they might react. We're afraid we might be laughed at or our message rejected. I think it's very important to follow His guidance and direction and to become committed fishermen for the Lord Jesus Christ. When we do, God will bless.

Getting back to our text, it's very interesting to note that we are told not only that it was a large catch of fish, but in verse 11 (John 21), we are told the exact number—153. Why this is mentioned we can't really say for sure. Alexander, a very early church father of the New Testament church, said he felt the 100 referred to was a perfect number. Well, in one sense, we still operate that way. We equate 100 with a perfect score. There is also an indication of that in the Bible when it speaks of the seed bearing an abundant harvest. It speaks of some reproducing twenty fold, but the epitome is that some will bear one hundred fold. In other words, excellent. Alexander felt that the 50 meant those who would be brought to faith from the Jewish people (or the nation of Jews), and that the 3 referred to the Holy Trinity—Father, Son, and Holy Spirit.

There was a later interpretation by Jerome, who translated the Bible into Latin. He said it described the 153 different kinds of fish (of course, now we know there are more than that). He felt that it meant that there would be people from every land and nation and race who would be brought into the net of salvation to heaven.

What does it really mean? The truth of the matter is that no one knows why the number is there. What is more important is to notice that in the second half of the sentence (v. 11), it says the net was not torn. Now, you'll remember that on another occasion, a different miracle happened when the disciples were fishing and the Lord gave them such an abundant catch of fish that the ship began to sink. You'll also remember that they had to call for another boat to come to the rescue, and they filled both with fish. And there was no problem with the net ripping either.

I like that analogy most of all because we are comparing this to the net of the holy Christian church. Whoever is caught in that net and brought to the Lord Jesus Christ, can feel security and comfort in knowing that there are not going to be accidental rips or that some of the catch will spill over the sides or slip out so they won't be saved. We who are fishermen for the Lord and who work for His church, bringing people by the power of God's Holy Spirit, can assure those who believe in Jesus Christ that they are safely within the net of the church. Those who believe will be given the gift of eternal salvation. That perfect number will be with God forever. All those who believe in Jesus Christ for their salvation will have eternal life before God's throne. They will be the perfect number of God's elect and will live eternally with Him in heaven.

Become a fisherman of the Lord and go out with the net of His Gospel. Bring people to Christ. Let's work together to do great things for the glory of our God!

38

Exclusive

When you have an *exclusive* story, it means you're the reporter who has the "scoop," you got the story first. If you have an *exclusive* gem, it's one of a kind. When you have an *exclusive* anything, it implies there is only one. Nothing else can compare.

Now what I want you to realize is that *God says He is exclusive.* He is one of a kind. He is not to be one choice from among many. He is not in any way prepared to share His glory with any false deity. He is *exclusive*—the one and only true God.

A portion of Scripture that speaks about all the nations knowing this one true God is found in Is. 55:1–9. Specifically, verse 5 says that all nations shall come to know Him, and that this God, who reveals Himself, is the one and only true God. Verses 8–9 say His thoughts are so far above our thoughts and His ways are so far above our ways, that there is no way we can understand Him nor comprehend Him. He is *exclusive.* He is not merely a better one of us. He is separate and different. He is God!

In the world we have a lot of people trying to tell us, "That is *too exclusive.*" They use the word *narrow.* They say, "My goodness, the Christian faith is narrow. You say there is only one God, and you say you have to believe in that one God in order to be saved?" Our answer: This is correct. But we didn't make this exclusivity. God Himself did.

The Christian church is not a man-made religion attempting to compete with other religions. Any intelligent person can study these other religions and see what they say. We can understand what the Unitarian church is saying. We can understand what the Hindu faith teaches. You can understand what the Bahai religion teaches as well as others. They say, "We are all heading for the same place and just happen to be on different roads, but in the end, all roads lead to the same place." That is simply *not* true!

It is a philosophy that appeals to man. It certainly is a humanistic view in the sense that man would like to think that as long as he is trying, God will somehow acknowledge that and say, "They didn't get it quite right, but they get an 'A' for effort." In the process, He is supposed to wink at all the errors and say, "As long as they were trying, and as long as they were making an effort, I guess I'll accept them."

While that sounds good to the human ear and to the human philosopher, it is not what God says. Theology is *not* an attempt to find out what man thinks about God. The best way to label these false teachings is to call them philosophy—man's search for God.

Theology is God revealing Himself to man. The theologian does not poll people to get their view of God, then take their consensus and say that is theology. What he does is quite different indeed. He goes to Scripture and finds there what God says about Himself. Based upon that authority, he then proclaims the God who has revealed Himself through His Son, Jesus. That is the basis of theology.

While it is true that in the Christian church there are differences of interpretations and differences of understanding as to what the Scriptures mean on various subjects, the name "Christian" implies *basic* agreement by all those who follow Christ. Christians believe God is a Triune God, and that He has revealed Himself as Father, Son, and Holy Spirit. His Son was sent to this earth in human form (the whole message of Christmas) in order to suffer and die in our place. Through that death and ultimate resurrection of the Lord on the third day, we have forgiveness of our sins. Through faith in Him, we have the promise of eternal life. These truths are the foundation of our Christian faith. It *is* exclusive. It *is* narrow. There is no other way to be saved! God says so!

Being exclusive, narrow, or specific is not necessarily negative. Let me point out a few examples. Suppose you went to a doctor in whom you had confidence. He diagnosed your illness and gave you a prescription. On this prescription, this piece of paper you are to take to the drugstore, are written instructions for the pharmacist to follow. Now, when you get to the drugstore and walk over to the drug counter, what do you say? Do you say, "Well, I'll tell you what. You have a couple hundred bottles there, and I'm sure they're all good. So just give me a few pills from each of them." You wouldn't consider doing that, would you? You *specifically* want what the doctor prescribed for your illness. You are not going to let the pharmacist mix it up or take something from any bottle he or she happens to choose. You will be very narrow in your request. You want just what that prescription says.

Or let's say you go into a grocery store. In the United States there are some pretty strict packaging regulations. If a package says "one pound," there is supposed to be one pound of rice, or coffee, or fruit in the package. No one buys, "a pound" of coffee and then at the checkout counter says, "I really don't care if it's only a half or three-quarters of a pound, I'll pay for a pound anyway." Do we take that attitude? I'll say not! We are very *specific*. If we are paying for one pound of coffee, we want one pound of coffee. Nothing more. Nothing less. One pound. That is what we are buying.

Let's say you're a busy person who must keep to a schedule. You have an appointment to meet someone at a restaurant at noon. How would you feel if you had to wait until 2 p.m. and then have the person casually stroll in? You'd say, "Where have you been? We were supposed to meet at noon." You wouldn't expect him or her to say, "Oh well, I know you said noon, but what's an hour or two? Does it matter?" You'd say, "It certainly does! I've been waiting here since noon." When we say noon, we mean noon—not two hours later. We don't get sloppy with things like that, do we? We are *specific*.

Take another example from married life. Somebody says, "I believe faithfulness in a Christian marriage means that I stay with the woman I'm married to. I don't go running around having affairs with others." That's very *exclusive* and very *narrow*, isn't it? But it's God-pleasing! It is what God says in His Word.

Those are just a few illustrations from everyday life.

Now when people begin to talk about all roads leading to the same place, it may sound tolerant and very wonderful to the non-Christian ear. It may sound very compassionate to the person who *isn't* very committed to God, but *it is totally contrary to what God says.* He is not going to share His glory with false Gods. There is *one* true God, and He *alone* is to be worshiped. His Son, Jesus Christ, is the only Messiah, the only Savior. He will not share that honor and glory with false "messiahs" or false "saviors."

So here is an exclusive message for God's people in His Word. It is spelled out in detail so that all can understand, all can see, all can be aware. There is *one* way to escape hell, *one* way to have the gift of eternal life, *one* way to get rid of sin, and that is through Jesus Christ, our Lord and Savior! This message is the *only* message that saves and the *only* message that has the power of God's Holy Spirit. It's the *only* message that converts.

39

Commitment

If you are a member of a Christian church, I am sure that there have been occasions when your pastor has asked you to talk to others about Christ. You may have found yourself very reluctant and hesitant, or even said, "I can't do that."

Well, I'd like to direct your attention to a man in the Bible—Jeremiah—who said the same thing. Together we are going to consider a dialogue between Jeremiah and God and see what God has to say about his reaction. The dialogue begins in Jer. 1:4. Jeremiah says, "God said to me, 'I knew you before you were formed within your mother's womb. Before you were born, I sanctified you and appointed you as My spokesman to the world.'" Jeremiah answers, "Oh, Lord God, I can't do that. I'm far too young; I am only a young person." In verse 7, we see God answer again. "Don't say that, for you will go wherever I send you and speak whatever I tell you." Then in verse 8, comes the promise. "And don't be afraid of the people, because I, the Lord, will be with you and see you through."

Some find excuses for not speaking about Christ to other people. I think we have to keep some things in mind. First of all, this subject is not new. It has been the mission of Christianity since the Pentecostal experience detailed in Acts 2. That chapter describes the birth of the Christian church and the work of the Holy Spirit in bringing people to faith in Jesus Christ. Someone had to put you in touch with Jesus. Maybe it was your Christian father or mother, maybe it was a grandparent, a neighbor, a friend, a stranger, a radio broadcast, or a gospel tract that someone gave you. But in some way or manner, someone had to tell you about Jesus.

We frequently get confused about the methods of telling others about Christ.

I certainly am among those pastors who feel that a strong, effective outreach is one involving two Christian people who, after prayer and training, go out in the name of the Lord and make a concerted effort (a discipline, so to speak) to contact people and invite them to receive Jesus Christ as their personal Savior.

Now, there are many people who feel that perhaps that is too direct. They don't like the idea of going up to someone's door and ringing the bell. I think we have to be cautious that we do not say legalistically that it has to be done in any certain way. We cannot demand that they follow any certain format or use any certain method. Our *lives* are to be the "witness." We may have different ideas and different opinions as to how we can most effectively witness for the Lord. The main point is not to get wrapped up in the method or the manner of doing it, but rather to concentrate on the fact that it *gets done*.

Proper motivation (which we see God using here with Jeremiah) is that we *remember* what God has done for us. God says to him, "I knew you; I redeemed you; I forgave you." It is the knowledge and the belief and the faith that God loves us that prompts and motivates us to go out in His name and witness to the world. It is a confession to the world that we have found something that we need and are excited about. And because it has helped us, we want to share with others who also need what we have found.

Now notice that God is the one who does the calling here. He had done many things before He called Jeremiah— He knew him; He delivered him; He redeemed him; He forgave him; and now God says, "I will also give you the words and the thoughts." God doesn't tell Jeremiah that He's able to use him because he's such a clever person and he's trained so hard and long. God isn't telling Jeremiah things like that. He is saying to him, "Go out and represent Me, My way of salvation. My message is what should be on your mouth."

That singlemindedness, that focus to never deviate was also true of St. Paul. It was not that he was clever, nor that he had wisdom, nor was he presenting certain little formulas of salesmanship. One of the most disgusting books I have seen in a long time is called, "Christ Was an Ad Man." If that isn't blasphemous, you tell me what is. The author tries to make it appear as though Jesus was a salesman trying to sell Himself to people. We do not "sell" Jesus Christ like soap or cereal; we are *inviting* those who will find no other way of salvation to recognize Him as their personal Savior. We proclaim that message, and it is by God's own power and the Holy Spirit's action that conversion takes place.

Now that is a tremendous challenge—to go out in the name of the Lord and talk to relatives, friends, co-workers, and even strangers. Our first reaction is very typical. Just like Jeremiah, we say, "I can't do that." He offered a pretty legitimate excuse, didn't he? He was too young, and he felt he had not been properly trained. Well, think of the excuses today. Perhaps you're thinking, "I wouldn't know what to say." As a pastor, I think I've heard that one over a thousand times. And that is just what it is, an excuse. Because God comes right back and says, "Don't say that. I've asked you to go, and I want you to go. I've asked you to speak, and I'm going to tell you what to say. I'm going to give you the words." If you read on in this first chapter of Jeremiah, you'll see that He spells that out in even more detail.

God doesn't promise, however, that He is going to create a situation without any complications or embarrassment. But He does give us complete and wonderful assurance when He says, "I will never leave you or forsake you. I will give you the words to say." Whatever the problem, whatever the need, whatever the consequence, whatever the ridicule, whatever the persecution, if you are representing God, and saying what He wants you to say in proclaiming the Good News that Jesus Christ is the Savior of the world, He will be with you. He will see you through. "Lo, I am with you always" (Matt. 28:20).

You really have to put yourselves on the line! You really have to make a *commitment*. You really have to make a decision! It is very clear that God had a reason for giving you faith and saving you. It's not confusing at all. We are told in His Word what His purpose is so that we will glorify Him and witness about Him to others. Every blessing, talent, and gift that He has given you is to enable you to use them to His glory as you proclaim His holy Word. Your mind, your energy, and your work (which provides a livelihood) are His instruments *so that you can do His work*. We so often get that confused. We think we are here just to live and work. We miss the whole point. Our life and our income are to sustain us so that we can do the *real work* of proclaiming the Gospel to the world. *Will you go and speak, or stand still and offer excuses?* May God motivate you with His promise of comfort and assurance to go out in His name. Speak to as many people as you can about Christ, and bear witness to your faith in Him. He will enable you to grow and to glorify the name of Jesus Christ in all that you do and say!

40

Witness

In John 1:19, we read about John the Baptist and his witness to Jesus Christ as the Savior of the world.

Think about the situation that John the Baptist was in. He had been preaching on the banks of the Jordan River. Many people had been coming out to listen to him. He was a powerful preacher, no doubt, and he also must have been somewhat of a curiosity because of his living style, clothes, and eating habits. (Read Mark 1:6.)

The officials of the Jewish people were becoming very upset. They decided to send a delegation to find out just who this man was, what he was preaching about, and what his goals were. First, they asked John, "Who are you." In verse 20 we read John's answer, "I am not the Messiah" (TEV).

Everyone was waiting for the Christ, or Messiah, which means "the anointed one," the One who was to come to be the Savior. It would have been quite a temptation for John the Baptizer to call himself the Messiah because the people were in a sense asking him, "Are you the one we are supposed to follow and worship?"

On a human level it could have been very tempting for John to respond affirmatively. He may have really struggled with that. Then they asked, "Well, then who are you? You must be someone important. Could you be Elijah?" But he replied, "I am not." Then they asked, "Are you the prophet?" (referring to Moses). He answered, "No."

"Well, then who are you?" they questioned. John the Baptist's reply is recorded in verses 26 and 27. "I am the one who baptizes with water. But right here in the crowd is someone whom you have never met, who will soon begin His ministry among you. And I am not even fit to untie His shoe."

This teaches us something. We have to swallow our pride. We must put down our own efforts at seeking honor, or some kind of acclaim, if we truly want to point people to Jesus Christ. I recognize that there is pride in all of us, and we all like to be acknowledged for what we do. We all like to have the feeling that what we do is appreciated. However, if we are going to direct people to Jesus Christ, then we have to uphold Him instead of ourselves. We have to point clearly to Him so that people see past us and see Jesus Christ. *He* has to be the focus. *He* has to be the goal.

We see here another simple lesson. John saw Jesus walking by (v. 29), stopped everything, and said, "Look! There He goes! That one is the Lamb of God who takes away the sin of the world!" There are many Christians who wonder whether or not they are able to witness. In an effort to get people to realize that they *can* witness for the Lord, there are all kinds of training courses and methods offered. The church has spent much time and effort trying to convince people that they should go out in the name of Jesus Christ and communicate with the world. We have made great progress through radio and television. The Christian church is reaching millions and millions of people. People all over the world speak about Jesus Christ to His honor and glory, and are bringing God's Word to the world.

But how about witnessing to your neighbor or your relative who is not close to God and possibly doesn't even have a relationship with Him? I believe it is important for you to read again John 1:29. Even if you are not well-trained, even if you are not well-educated, even if you do not have some system of remembering Bible verses or know an outline, you can at least do what John the Baptizer did. You can say, "There is Jesus Christ, the Lamb of God." You can point people to Jesus. That is something you *can* do. Anyone can do it. I believe that is the first basic element in witnessing. You say to the person, "I want you to see Jesus Christ. I want to hold up Jesus Christ for you to see. I want you to recognize who

He is. I believe that He is God's own Son, true God, and I want you to believe that too."

The least thing that any Christian can do is what John the Baptizer did here. When people are seeking, when they are asking questions, when they are searching, point them to Jesus and say, "Behold the Lamb of God." As you grow in your confidence while God's Holy Spirit works in you, you will want to say more, and you will want to make your witness as effective as you can by defining what the "Lamb of God" means.

In the Old Testament a lamb was offered, or sacrificed for the sins of people. It would not take very much effort for you to prepare a few sentences to explain this. For instance, "When I say, *Lamb of God*, I want you to understand that Jesus (Lamb of God) was the sacrifice for you and all humanity. The Old Testament priests sacrificed a lamb on an altar, but now God doesn't want that kind of sacrifice—He wants our hearts. God's own Son gave Himself as the one-time sacrifice and paid for the sins of the whole world. The sinless Lamb of God took our sins upon Himself, and through His blood we are washed clean. He came to live here on earth. He sacrificed Himself. He died in our place. Because of Him we are free from our sins when we believe in Him as our Savior."

Then you can give a personal witness about what Jesus means to you. What does it mean to you that your sins are forgiven? What does it mean to you to know that you have eternal life? The whole idea of your witness is to express what you know and believe and what you have experienced—the joy, peace, serenity, and strength—because of your faith and trust in the Lamb of God.

Your goal in life as a Christian should be twofold: (1) fight all temptations to become self-centered and focus attention away from yourself toward Christ; and (2) become strong in pointing to Him. Your witness may be very simple at first— just showing Jesus to people. Later, as you grow in faith and in the Word, you will be able to expand on that and say more and more about who Jesus is, what He has done, and what He means to you.

41

Victorious

This new life we have in Jesus Christ should result in victorious living. You know, we have far too many people in the Christian church who claim to be followers of Jesus Christ and yet are gloomy people. This kind of dull, lifeless attitude makes it appear as though they are leading an unhappy life—certainly not one filled with excitement.

Suppose you were an unbeliever, and you met a Christian like I just described. What would you think of such a "Christian" example? You'd have every reason to say, "Well, being a Christian certainly can't be much fun—there certainly isn't much victory to it."

To make matters even worse, unbelievers so often see a lovelessness among Christians. The very mark of a believer should be love—love toward one another. But instead of love, we often see conflict. Even within Christian congregations, we see factions rising and opposing one another. Consequently, the congregation is unable to cooperate to do the very basic work of God that it has been called to do. So the unbeliever says, "Well, who needs it."

If you're in the doldrums, experiencing one of those negative moods in your Christian life, take a look at another one of those key chapters of the Bible—the sixth chapter of St. Paul's letter to the church at Rome.

Romans 6 deals with the new life we have in Jesus Christ, and it is to be a victorious life. I hope you'll read this chapter. In the opening verses Paul stresses two important doctrines that assure us of this new life in Jesus Christ.

First of all, he refers to the death of Jesus and states that through His death we have the forgiveness of all our sins.

Jesus Christ has paid the penalty for our sins and because He died in our place, we now have the certainty, if we believe in Him as our personal Savior, that our sins have been forgiven. Paul relates this to Baptism and says that in Jesus Christ we in our sinful human nature are dead and buried. We are no longer slaves to sin. We are no longer under the control of sin.

Secondly, a new life takes place. Just as Jesus rose from the dead, so within us there is a new life by the power of God—through the gift of His Holy Spirit working in us—we are to have a resurrected life.

So there is the "old man," the old sinful self which is to be daily put to death in remembrance that our sins are forgiven through Jesus Christ. Then there is the new man—the new life, the spiritual life within us that is to grow daily and become strong in the power of Jesus living within us. Obviously, we never achieve perfection during our daily struggle. We are still living here on earth, still influenced by Satan, and there are going to be sins in our lives. But we should strive toward that goal. We should grow and improve. We should want to follow Christ, to live for Him, and to refuse to let Satan dominate and control us.

> *Rom. 6:12–13:* Sin must no longer rule in your mortal bodies, so that you obey the desires of your natural self. Nor must you surrender any part of yourselves to sin to be used for wicked purposes. Instead, give yourselves to God, as those who have been brought from death to life, and surrender your whole being to Him to be used for righteous purposes (TEV).

In this new life, we are to turn from those things that violate God's will. In Prov. 6:16 there is a list of seven things "the Lord hates and cannot tolerate" (TEV). Let's look at three of them:

A proud look. Could it be that pride is keeping you from victorious living? In your own smug way you think you are better than other people and this is alienating them and turning them against you. Maybe it is your pride that needs to be yielded to God.

A lying tongue. Does your mouth run out of control? Do you cut people down and tell lies about them that harm their reputations? Maybe it's your tongue that's keeping you from experiencing the victorious life that God wants you to have.

A mind that thinks up wicked plans. So frequently people want to reserve their minds for themselves so they can think about evil things. Your whole mind must be committed to God if you want to experience some really victorious living.

There are two other Bible references I'd like to point out to you regarding victorious living. In 1 Thess. 4:3–5, Paul says that God expects us to live lives free from sexual immorality. I'm convinced that sexual immorality is what's keeping many people from finding the true meaning and happiness that comes from following Jesus Christ in a committed way.

In Philippians 2, Paul says that as Christians we should have the same attitude that Christ Jesus had. He goes on to explain that if your attitude is constantly negative, if you're always pessimistic, your life won't be victorious. All Christians should have confidence that Jesus Christ is by their side and that they belong to Him. Therefore, we should be able to put negativism and pessimism behind us and say that it was part of our sinful nature.

Please examine every part of your life. You may discover that there are things that have to be turned over to Christ in order for you to be able to celebrate and daily live the victorious life of faith.

42

Comfort

Each Christmas season should be a time of joy for all of us. As a matter of fact, many of the songs and carols talk about it as being the season to be jolly, the season to be merry.

Well, the truth of the matter is that each year around Christmas we read reports that this is, in fact, a season of sorrow and sadness for many people. For some people the feelings of loneliness and bereavement cause them to have despair during the holiday season. This seems to contradict the fact that this should be a season of joy.

Now, let's look at this situation a little bit and see if we can analyze what the problem is. To begin with, we have to be realistic—there are many problems in this world. And even though it's Christmas, those problems continue to exist. The people who've lost their loved ones still have bereavement. The people in pain still have their pain. On top of all the personal problems that people face—the problems of loneliness, sorrow, sickness—there are the world problems that have an impact on every one of us.

There is the threat of nuclear holocaust hanging over all of us. Certainly the young people realize that danger. Perhaps they realize the danger more than we adults do. And as more and more nations acquire the know-how to build nuclear weapons the danger increases.

There is danger of the weapons being used unintentionally and accidently. We used to worry about a world leader making a mistake and accidently pushing the button, so to speak, that would plunge us into nuclear war. Well, now the danger is far more serious because it's getting to the point where it is beyond human control. Computers are playing an ever increasing role in our nuclear defense systems. The human mind is just not capable of thinking quickly enough in a nuclear emergency to analyze the problems of lining up the missiles, calculating the destructive powers, figuring out which targets to hit, and so on. Everything is computerized, and we know that computers can fail.

Remember some years ago when they had the blackout on the East Coast due to a computer failure? Some of our space shuttle launches have been delayed because of computer problems. And those of you who have to rely on a computer at work know they often fail. The point is computers can fail. That is why I believe our young people are getting so upset about potential nuclear war. They realize that it could happen accidently due to computer failure. Now that is really alarming!

So, in addition to the worry and concern that our grandparents had with the everyday problems of losing a job, declaring bankruptcy, fighting with an illness or pain, death in the family, etc., today we also have these overwhelming world problems hanging over us and causing us additional worry and concern. There is plenty to be troubled about today.

How in the world can a person say that Christmas is a time to rejoice, to be happy, to be merry? Just think of the problems you face. Are you frazzled? at your wits' end? financially hassled? We just reviewed how many problems there are in today's world, and there is no joy in those, is there? However, if you look in the right place, you'll find joy even in the midst of suffering. You'll find joy even in the middle of all your problems—a joy that will surpass even the worries and the troubled concerns of the world in which you're living because your joy will come from God.

I would like to refer you to a chapter of Scripture that talks about joy. The prophet Isaiah gives a beautiful record of what this joy is supposed to be in chapter 61. I hope that you will read the entire chapter. I would like to focus on verse 10. He says, "I will greatly rejoice in the Lord, my soul shall exalt in my God." Here is the reason: "He has clothed me in garments of salvation."

Let's look at that verse for a moment. Why was Isaiah

willing to rejoice even though he had many of the same problems we have today? He was willing to rejoice and able to rejoice because he knew that God had clothed him in the garments of salvation. You see he was looking beyond this life. He realized there *is* hope. He says he doesn't have to settle for just what is here and now, but he can be assured that he is saved.

You know that the ultimate problem in all of our lives is the confusion of wondering where we are going, what is going to happen to us, and is there life after death? In Is. 61:10 all those questions are answered. He says in effect, "Of course there is." Not only that, but God has assured me that I am saved. That's why he is rejoicing. He goes on to say that God has covered me with the robe of righteousness. God has made everything right. He has forgiven all of our sins through His Son Jesus Christ.

Now, if you believe in Jesus Christ as your personal savior, then you are covered and washed clean in His blood. You are covered in His righteousness. That means that you are right with God. All of your sin and all of your guilt have been washed away. No wonder there can be rejoicing when you look at Christ.

The point is this: Where are you looking for your comfort? If you are looking to the world, you won't find it. There is no lasting comfort that the world can give. But if you look to Christ, you will find it. For He has given you salvation and He has given you forgiveness. So rejoice in that knowledge and be happy.

43

Littleness

So often we think in terms of big things. We talk about wealthy individuals or about corporations that are very big and powerful. Jesus told us that whoever should be greatest among you, let him be your servant. He has reversed our whole understanding of who is big and who is mighty. He has put down the mighty and elevated those who are of poor esteem and those who perhaps the world would look down upon.

There are so many ways that we could get into this topic of littleness, but the Bible verse I'd like to focus on is Prov. 30:28. I almost hesitate to use this particular verse because the Hebrew is a little difficult to understand. The King James version translates it the way I'd like to use it for this discussion.

Prov. 30:28: "The spider taketh hold with her hands, and is in kings' palaces" (KJV).

Spiders are interesting creatures. A spider doesn't need a cheering audience when it does its work. As a matter of fact, a spider usually does its work under a stairwell, in a damp basement, or someplace where it's all by itself. And it does its work diligently and fervently. I think we can learn from the spider's example.

I like that thought of the spider working quietly all by itself and not needing the applause of others. So often people are eager to be recognized and want the accolades and the acclaim of a large audience. But God recognizes the quiet souls who are willing to serve Him in a committed way even when not recognized by their fellowman.

Another thing I like about spiders is they're diligent. Have you ever seen an unfinished spider web? Well, I'll bet not very many. If the spider is left alone, and continues to live, it's going to finish its web. Now that's diligence.

It would be very good for us to be more diligent in the way in which we serve the Lord. We need to work diligently and fervently without giving up. So often we have beautiful ideas. We get started on a wonderful project and then some little obstacle gets in our way and we give up. We say, "Well, I guess it's not worth the effort."

One other thing about spiders that occurs to me is how beautiful their webs are. I recall seeing a huge web in the Florida Everglades years ago. The spider had woven it between tree branches, and when I spotted it, the sun was shining on it. It was just beautiful! The geometrical design was perfect. You couldn't find a tapestry woven in the Middle Ages that would be any prettier.

That reminds me that anything we do for the Lord ought to be worth doing well. That doesn't mean you have to spend a lot of money, but it should be done neatly. Whatever it is you're doing, it should be done as well as you can do it to glorify God.

I feel that the little things in life need to receive more attention from us. Things like a little snowflake or a little seed that we plant in the ground. You know how Jesus looked at simple things. He would take a piece of grain and comment on it. Or He would call a little child to His side and remind us that our faith needs to be childlike—simple and really committed and full of trust.

On one occasion when Jesus was going to heal a blind man, He chose to use spit. We all know that Jesus could have just spoken a word and the man would have been healed of his blindness. But He chose to take spittle from His mouth and use it to heal.

I think of the sacraments in the Christian church that God has given us. What does God choose to use in Baptism to fill with the power of His Word? He uses water. Isn't it extraordinary of God to use an ordinary thing like water? In the sacrament of Holy Communion, where we receive the body and blood of Jesus Christ for our spiritual nourishment, what did God choose to use? He didn't choose to use something made from an exotic formula. Instead, He chose to use simple things—unleavened bread and wine.

If God has the power, as He has all power, to take tiny and insignificant things and use them in a big majestic way, then there is hope for us, isn't there?

We all know what we deserve. We deserve nothing but His judgment—not only here, but eternally. But God chose to send His Son, Jesus Christ, to save us. Through the coming of His Son to our world, through His dying on the cross, through His resurrection from the dead, and through His presence in our lives as our resurrected Lord, He has transformed us into His children.

As a result of that transformation, we are filled with God's power. When God chooses to use us as His witnesses to others, His spirit is at work converting and transforming people's lives.

The next time you see a spider remember that even these little insignificant creatures can teach us some lessons about life. Remember to do the Lord's work diligently, to work without the applause of your fellowman, and to do the best work you are capable of doing to the glory of God.